PRAYER ARDENT OPENS HEAVEN'S GATE.

GRADUATED SUNDAY-SCHOOL TEXT-BOOKS,
No. III.

BIBLE MORALITY;

OR,

ELEMENTS OF MORAL SCIENCE.

FOR SUNDAY-SCHOOLS.

BY JAMES FLOY, D.D.

New York:
PUBLISHED BY CARLTON & PORTER,
SUNDAY-SCHOOL UNION, 200 MULBERRY-STREET.

PREFACE.

The last General Conference of the Methodist Episcopal Church directed the publication of a series of graduated text-books adapted to a regular course of study in our Sunday-schools.

That series will consist of seven separate volumes in the following order:

I. The Old Testament History.

II. The New Testament History.

III. Bible Morality; or, the Elements of Moral Science.

IV. Doctrines and Institutions of Christianity.

V. Sacred Geography.

VI. The Evidences of Christianity.

VII. Church History.

The present volume, it will be seen, is the third of the series. Its object is to teach the elements of morality, as derived from the Scriptures, in a manner adapted to the young. Simplicity and directness of style and language have been aimed at, and almost every point is illustrated by anecdote or story.

As is intended to be the case with the other volumes of the series, the present is designed to occupy just twelve months when studied by classes in the Sunday-school. There are fifty-two lessons, one for each week in the year; but it will be observed that at the end of each quarter a lesson is given which is simply a revision of the studies of the preceding three months. Thus, if a class begin the book on the first Sunday in January, as is recommended, and as is supposed will be the case with each volume of the series when it is completed, the days for quarterly revision will be the last Sabbaths in the months of March, June, September, and December. Hence the lesson for any particular day may readily be found; and if the plan be carried out, the scholars in all our schools will be engaged on the same subject at the same time. Of course it is not to be understood that the teachers will be confined to the questions found in the book, either at the close of each lesson or at the end of the quarter. Any others may be asked, and sometimes it may be found profitable to let the scholars ask questions and the teacher answer.

The other volumes of the series are in course of preparation, and will appear in due time.

CONTENTS.

INTRODUCTORY.

"I AM sure," said little Annie to her mother, "I am sure I can never learn this lesson. It is too hard, and there are so many words in it that I do not know the meaning of."

"It is rather difficult," replied her mother, "but I am surprised to hear my daughter say she *cannot* learn it. If you should say, 'I will not learn it,' or, 'I will not try to learn it,' or, 'I will not study it'"—

"O mother," said Annie, interrupting her, "I would not say that; I do not mean that. Brother and I both intend to try to learn it; but it does seem very hard, and these long words puzzle us both."

Her mother, having herself read the book through, assured her daughter that she would find it easier and more interesting as she proceeded, especially if she thoroughly committed to memory the first lesson.

Being thus encouraged, Annie and her brother began to study in

ANNIE AND HER MOTHER.

earnest, and before the end of the week they could not only answer the questions at the end of the chapter, but repeat every word of it without hesitation.

My dear young reader, *you can do so too if you will.* Resolve to learn it. Don't give it up, and you will certainly succeed. If you are not willing to make this resolution, I suppose you will not know much more about it next Sunday than you do to-day. But I hope you will determine to do as did Annie and her brother; and if you do, you will overcome all difficulties as certainly and as easily as they did.

BIBLE MORALITY;

OR,

ELEMENTS OF MORAL SCIENCE.

LESSON FIRST.

DEFINITIONS.

In every science there are certain principles or truths which are admitted without argument. In the mathematics, for instance, it is considered as an axiom, or self-evident truth, that the whole is greater than any of its parts; and in chemistry it is assumed that matter cannot be destroyed. So in the study upon which we now enter there are certain primary truths, which need no argument to establish them. That there is a God, that he has revealed himself and made known his will to man, and that this revelation is contained in the holy Scriptures, are taken for granted as facts about which there can be no dispute. They are the *axioms* of moral science.

Science is knowledge properly arranged. It is the result of the experience and study of many minds, condensed and classified for the benefit of individuals.

The various branches of science may be arranged in three divisions, physical, natural, and moral. In one or other of these divisions we include all subjects of scientific study.

The *physical sciences* are confined to objects destitute of animal life. Agriculture, botany, and chemistry belong to this division. So also navigation, mathematics, astronomy, and kindred subjects may be included among the physical sciences.

Under the head of *natural science* we class those studies which pertain to animated, as distinguished from inanimate nature. Birds, beasts, fishes, and insects of every variety, with their structure, habits, and instincts, form the subjects of natural science. Mental philosophy, which treats of the human mind, is also included in this division.

Moral science is exclusively confined to the moral nature of rational creatures. It regards human beings as possessed of reason and conscience, as accountable for their actions, and as subjects of praise or blame for those actions hereafter as well as in the present life.

Hence it is not easy to over-estimate the importance of the study of moral science. Man's moral nature is superior to that which he possesses in common with the brute creation, and the relative importance of this study may be found in the difference between the present life, by which all other studies are bounded, and that endless existence, including the present and the future, which makes up the field for the investigations of moral science.

Questions on Lesson I.

1. What is said of every science?
2. What is an axiom?
3. Give a mathematical axiom.
4. What is assumed as a principle in chemistry?
5. Name some of the primary truths in moral science.
6. Give a definition of science.
7. From what does science result?
8. Why are those results condensed and classified?

9. In how many divisions may the sciences be arranged?
10. What are they?
11. What may be included in these divisions?
12. To what are the physical sciences confined?
13. Name some studies which belong to the physical sciences.
14. In which division do we include astronomy, etc.?
15. What subjects fall into the division of natural science?
16. In which division do we place mental philosophy?
17. Of what does mental philosophy treat?
18. To what is moral science exclusively confined?
19. How does it regard human beings?
20. What makes the study of moral science so important?

LESSON SECOND.

REASON AND CONSCIENCE.

A RATIONAL creature is one who is possessed of reason, and reason is that faculty of the mind by which we are enabled to distinguish between truth and error, and by the exercise of which we gain knowledge.

If Peter is told that twice two are five, or that it takes three halves of an apple to make a whole one, his reason contradicts the statement, and he says it is not true. An infant or an idiot would not be able to detect the error. Hence we say of an infant, his reasoning faculty is not yet developed; and of an idiot, he is not a rational creature.

Instinct in brutes, in some respects, resembles reason in man. But instinct never discerns between what is true and what is false, and never discovers any new truth. The nests of birds, the hut of the beaver, and the ingeniously constructed web of the spider, are the same as they have always been. One generation of beasts or birds makes no improvement upon the preceding; and although the shape in which bees build their cells is the best that even reason could devise, no one supposes that bees could vary that shape at their pleasure, or that they have any conception of the superiority of a hexagon over other mathematical figures.

A limit cannot be assigned to the reasoning faculty. We know that by exercise its powers are increased. We know, too, that at best human reason is imperfect, and that without some higher guide the wisest of men may be led astray, and mistake error for truth, and truth for error.

Conscience, sometimes called the moral sense, is a faculty possessed by all rational creatures. Its office is to determine between right and wrong. When we obey its dictates, conscience is a source of pleasure; when we disobey, it produces uneasiness and mental disquiet.

If Peter should be tempted to strike his little sister, and before doing it should stop to think, something within him would say, "It is wrong to do so." That something is conscience. It would in effect say, "Don't strike her." But if he did not stop to think, or if after thinking he should give way to his angry passion, his conscience would trouble him. He would feel bad. He would know that he had been doing wrong.

But now, on the other hand, if, while playing with his dog, the dog should bite Peter, or if a vicious horse should kick him, we might be disposed to blame, and perhaps to punish, both the dog and the horse; but nobody supposes that either of them would feel bad on account of what he had done. We could not say that either had done any moral wrong, because neither dogs, nor horses, nor other dumb animals, have any conscience or moral sense.

Paul the apostle describes the working of this faculty in the following verses:

"For when the Gentiles, which have not the law, do by nature the things contained in the law, these having not the law, are a law unto themselves: which show the work of the law written in their hearts, their conscience also bearing witness, and their thoughts the meanwhile accusing, or else excusing one another."—Rom. ii, 14, 15.

Questions on Lesson II.

1. What is meant by a rational creature?
2. What does reason enable us to do?
3. What may be gained by the exercise of reason?
4. How do we know that twice two are not five?
5. How many halves make a whole one?
6. Why does not an infant know that?
7. What do we say of an idiot?
8. What, in brutes, resembles reason in man?
9. What is instinct incapable of discerning?
10. What does instinct never reveal?
11. How is this illustrated?
12. Can you assign a limit to the reasoning faculty?
13. How are its powers increased?

14. Is human reason ever perfect?
15. What would be the result if we had no higher guide?
16. What is conscience sometimes called?
17. Who possess conscience?
18. What is the office of conscience?
19. When is conscience a source of pleasure?
20. What is the consequence when the dictates of conscience are disregarded?
21. How is this illustrated in the case of Peter and his sister?
22. Do we ever attribute moral wrong-doing to dumb animals?
23. Why not?
24. What does Paul say of conscience in Rom. ii, 14, 15?

LESSON THIRD.

MOTIVE, THE TEST OF ACTION.

In judging of any act with reference to its moral quality it is necessary to regard the *motive* of him who does it. In other words, before we can tell how much praise or blame is due we inquire why, or for what reason, was the act done?

Charlie broke a pane of glass. Charlie did wrong, and ought to be punished. Not so fast. Let us inquire how it happened, or why he broke it. It seems the whole family went to a meeting one night, and before it ended Charlie's mother was taken sick. She, with her little boy, was obliged to leave and go home. His father and the other members of the family did not miss them, or know they had left. When they reached home, which was a quarter of a mile from the meeting-house, they could not get in. The door was locked, and they had forgotten that Charlie's big brother had taken charge of the key. What shall we do? said the little boy. Shall I run back and get the key? His mother thought he had better do so; but first she went round through the garden to the back of the house, to try if they could not get in by that way. They found that the back door had been fastened on the inside. Near that door was a small window. "If I could get that window open," said Charlie, "I could reach the bolt and open the door." But the window was fast. "Perhaps," said his mother, "if you could break out a pane of glass you might put your hand through and unbolt the door." "O yes," said he, "I could do that."

So his mother, who began to feel very faint, told him to do it. Then Charlie with a stick broke a pane of glass, reached in his hand, unbolted the door, and they were soon in the warm house.

I will tell you about another boy who broke a pane of glass. His name was Frederic, but he was usually called Fred. His little sister Gertrude had a beautiful pet Canary bird which she loved very much, and so did all the family; he was such a cunning little fellow and sang so sweetly. They called him Cherub, and I really think he knew his name.

One afternoon Fred came home from school with his books strapped tightly together, and opening the parlor door the cat followed him. By some means Cherub had got out of his cage, and the cat seeing him on the table near the window made a spring at him. In a moment, without stopping to think, Fred hurled his books at the cat with such force that they went through a large pane of glass. There was a terrible crash. The whole family, who were up stairs, heard it, and were much frightened. So was Fred, and so was the cat, but Cherub looked calmly down from the top of his cage, to which he had flown; and, if he had known how to do it, I have no doubt he would have thanked Fred for saving him from the jaws of the cat even at the expense of a broken parlor window.

Another way of breaking a pane of glass is well known to boys who are fond of play. It is by accidentally knocking a ball through it; and yet another is to throw a stone at it intentionally, as a bad boy might be supposed to do in a fit of anger.

I must say I never knew a boy so bad as that; but if such a thing should be you would certainly be right in saying *he* ought to be punished.

Perhaps too you would be right in blaming the boys for carelessness, who broke a window accidentally while playing ball. They ought to pay the damage certainly, but their guilt is not like that of him who broke the pane of glass on purpose. I don't think any one would blame Fred very much. I know Gertrude kissed him, and called him a brave boy for saving her bird's life.

As to Charlie, of course he did what his mother told him, and nobody would think of blaming him. So you see here is the same act, breaking a window, done in four different ways, and the degree of blame depends in each case upon the motive or reason for the act, and not upon the act itself.

Questions on Lesson III.

1. In judging of a moral action what must be regarded?
2. What do we want to know before awarding praise or blame?
3. Tell me about Charlie and the broken pane of glass.
4. Did he deserve punishment for what he did?
5. Why not?
6. What is said about Frederic?
7. Did he do wrong in breaking the window?
8. Mention another method by which boys sometimes break windows.
9. Ought they to be blamed for carelessness?
10. What else ought they to do?
11. Who ought to be punished?
12. What is the fourth method here mentioned?
13. What ought to be done to such?
14. Why?
15. What makes the difference in the conduct of these boys?

LESSON FOURTH.

MOTIVE NOT ALWAYS A JUSTIFICATION.

It must not be inferred, from what has been said on the subject of motive, that actions in themselves wrong lose that character because done with a good intention.

In the first place, we do not always know the motive by which we are actuated in any given case. We may deceive ourselves, and we are specially liable to self-deception when inclination prompts us to do wrong. On the one hand, as I cannot see the heart of another, I am bound to judge of his conduct charitably. So also, as I know that I am in great danger of deceiving myself, I ought to be very jealous of the motives by which I profess to be governed.

Suppose a boy plays truant, and goes a fishing, when his parents think he is at school. Would it be satisfactory to his father and mother if, when found out, he should plead that his motive was to breathe a little fresh air, and that he felt the need of exercise? Would his teacher accept that as a sufficient excuse? Certainly not, and his own conscience would condemn him. He would doubt himself, just as everybody else would doubt the truth of the statement that to benefit his health was really the motive which actuated him in playing truant.

But secondly, even when satisfied that our motives are good, they will not justify us in doing what will injure others.

There was in the papers some time ago an account of the destruction of a man's property by a number of ladies. They justified themselves, and other people were disposed to justify them, because the property destroyed was ardent spirits. They said, "It is wrong for him to sell rum. Drunkards are made by it, and his business has been the means of producing much misery in the village." So one afternoon quite a large company, I think there were twenty, entered the rumseller's shop in a body, and while some of them held him fast, the rest stove in the heads of his casks, and emptied all his bottles into the street.

The intention of these ladies was good. They wanted to put a stop to a great evil. So far as we know, they had no selfish object in view; and yet it is probable not one of them went to sleep that night with a quiet conscience. Why? Because they did wrong; and the motive, though in itself laudable, did not justify them in destroying even a wicked man's property.

Suppose that, after effecting their work of destruction, these ladies had made up a purse, and paid the man the full value of his liquor. That would have been no more than right; but it would not have justified them in their conduct. Wicked as it was for him to sell liquor, and beneficial as it would have been to the community if he could have been restrained, that was not the proper way to do it, and their good motive was no justification for their conduct.

In the third place, we are all ignorant of the future. We cannot tell what will be the result of any course of conduct. Conscience tells us to do what is right now, and now to abstain from what is wrong. The good that we may suppose will follow from disobeying the voice of conscience may never come to pass. The result may be directly contrary to our expectations.

A physician who was called to visit a very sick man, saw that in all probability he had but a few hours to live. The doctor thought that the truth might hurry the man out of the world, and that a falsehood might assist the medicine and prolong his life. So he spoke cheeringly, and told him that he would get well. The consequence was that the will which the dying man had proposed to make just before the doctor entered was postponed, and what was infinitely worse, his preparation to meet his God was also postponed. Before the sun rose the next morning he passed away, leaving the lawyers to dispute about his property, and his friends in dreadful uncertainty as to his future state. It would have been better for them, better for the dead man, and better for the doctor, if he had told what he believed to be the truth on that occasion.

Questions on Lesson IV.

1. What is said of wrong actions done with a good intention?
2. Of what are we frequently ignorant?
3. When are we specially liable to self-deception?
4. Why should I judge charitably of another's conduct?
5. Why should I be jealous of my own motives?
6. What is said of the boy who played truant?

7. If our motives are really good, will they justify us in injuring others?
8. How is this illustrated?
9. Was the object of the ladies good?
10. Why did their consciences trouble them?
11. If they had paid for the liquor they destroyed, what then?
12. What is the third reason here given?
13. What does conscience tell us?
14. Why did not the doctor tell the sick man the truth?
15. What did he tell him?
16. What was the consequence?
17. What else was postponed?
18. When did the sick man die?
19. In what condition did he leave his friends?
20. For whom would it have been better if the doctor had told the truth?

LESSON FIFTH.

CONSCIENCE AS A RULE OF CONDUCT.

THE question, How far is conscience a safe rule of conduct? is a very important one. He who violates his conscience does wrong; but it does not follow that he who acts in accordance with his conscience always does right.

Let us illustrate these two statements. And first, he who violates his conscience always does wrong.

Patrick was brought up in a family where he was taught that it was wicked to eat flesh on Friday. On one occasion, when he was from home, a beef-steak was placed before him. Knowing what day of the week it was, but feeling hungry, he took a piece and ate it. Many other boys could have done so without feeling any condemnation, but Patrick did what he believed to be wrong. His conscience condemned him and he was unhappy.

Take another illustration of this truth. One day James was asked why his brother John was not at school. He told the teacher that John had been sent on an errand by his mother. While he said that his voice faltered, and his face was red as crimson. He thought he was telling an untruth. It so happened that John *had* been sent on an errand, although James did not know it, and he feared that his brother was playing truant.

James intended to tell a lie to deceive his teacher and to screen John. Because what he said happened to be true in fact, his guilt was none the less, and his conscience troubled him.

In all cases of this kind the path of duty is very plain. It is to shun whatever conscience tells us to shun, and we may rest assured that it is always safe not to do anything that violates conscience.

Whatever may be our opinion as to the guilt incurred by eating flesh-meat on Friday, all will agree that it would not have been morally wrong for Patrick to have refrained from it; and if James had said, in reply to his teacher's question, "I do not know," his conscience would not have troubled him. If he had even told his teacher what he feared, although he was under no obligation to do that, he would not have felt condemned, and his brother John would not have been injured.

But, on the other hand, while conscience is a safe guide as to what we may *not* do, it is not always right to *do* what conscience seems to sanction.

The parents of a little boy had taught him that it was not wrong to steal. The father and mother were both thieves. By their example as well as by their instruction they had impressed upon his youthful mind this dreadful lesson. He was detected in an attempt to commit a theft, and was sent to the House of Refuge, where he received religious instruction. He became a good boy, and grew up to be a useful member of society. In telling his early history he said that in those days his conscience did not condemn him for stealing, though he used to feel bad when he was found out.

So it has been with men as well as boys in all ages. Conscience has been perverted, and has made it seem right, in certain circumstances, to deceive, to persecute, and even to commit murder. The apostle Paul, previous to his conversion, is a memorable illustration of this truth. He persecuted the disciples of the Saviour, dragged men and women to prison, and was the occasion of putting many of them to death. He did all this, as he himself tells us, with a quiet conscience; but when he was made to see his error he repented and *obtained mercy, because he did those things ignorantly and in unbelief.* (1 Tim. 1, 13.)

Questions on Lesson V.

1. What is said to be an important question?
2. What of him who violates his conscience?
3. Is it always right to do what conscience dictates?
4. Relate the case of Patrick?
5. Why did Patrick's conscience condemn him?
6. Suppose he had not known that it was Friday, what then?
7. What reason did James give for his brother's absence?
8. Was that true?
9. Why did he blush and his voice falter?
10. Was his guilt as great as if he had stated what was false?
11. What is duty in cases like this?
12. What is always safe?
13. In the cases referred to what should Patrick have done?
14. What was the proper course for James?
15. Who taught the little boy to steal?
16. In what way did they teach that lesson?
17. What was the consequence of his being detected?
18. Why did not his conscience condemn him for stealing?
19. What has made it seem right to commit great crimes?
20. What is said of the apostle Paul?
21. Repeat what he says of himself in 1 Tim. i, 13.

LESSON SIXTH.

CONSCIENCE CONTINUED: THE STORY OF FRANK.

Conscience differs in different individuals; hence it cannot be a universal rule of action. Hence, too, what may be sin in one is not always sin in another. If you were to stop on your way to Sunday-school, and engage in a game of ball, your conscience would condemn you, and you would feel guilty.

But suppose other boys are there playing, and, on inquiring, you find that they have lately arrived from a foreign land, and that they do not know that it is the Lord's day, or that they have not been taught that it is wrong to play ball on Sunday, it is not likely that their consciences will condemn them.

Mary would feel guilty if she should hem her doll's apron on Sunday; but here is a little girl of the same age as Mary, whose conscience does not trouble her even when she spends the whole Sabbath in play. The reason is Mary's conscience is enlightened; the other girl's is not.

Sometimes conscience is perverted, as in the case of the boy mentioned in the last chapter, whose parents taught him that it was not wrong to steal. Instances of this kind are very rare. However bad a father or a mother may be, it is very seldom that either of them will teach a child so wicked a lesson.

More frequently conscience becomes dull, seared, and sometimes even deadened, by our own conduct; and this not all at once, but by degrees and almost insensibly.

At a day-school to which Frank went when quite a little boy, the teacher was in the habit of requiring each scholar to bring from home a written excuse for being absent from school.

One morning Frank was half way to the school-house before he remembered that he had been kept at home the day before. He turned back. "I must get Ma," said he, "to write me an excuse." On his way homeward he met one of the larger scholars, a boy whose name I will not mention. "Pshaw," said he, when told why Frank was going back, "why don't you write an excuse for yourself?" This question seemed so wicked that it frightened the little fellow, and he could give no answer.

"Stay," said the boy, "I will write one for you." So he sat down on a rock by the roadside, tore a blank leaf out of his geography, and with his pencil wrote: "Please excuse Frank for being absent yesterday." To this the wicked boy signed the name of Frank's mother. "There," said he, "take that and give it to the teacher."

Poor little Frank! His first impulse was to tear up the note, or throw it away. But, without saying anything, he put it in his pocket, and walked on with his companion.

They talked of various subjects, but Frank's thoughts were continually reverting to the note in his pocket. His conscience told him that he had been doing wrong to take it at all; that it would be right to destroy it, or give it back to the writer, and that to hand it to his teacher would be a complication of wickedness, involving deceit, falsehood, and even forgery.

Now in all this Frank was at perfect liberty to act as he pleased. He might do as his conscience told him, and regain his peace of mind; or pursue the opposite course and take the consequences. Two things are very clear: if he yields to the good impulse, he will gain a victory that will render future victories easy; if he disobeys the voice of conscience, he will disobey it with the more ease hereafter.

Questions on Lesson VI.

1. What is here said of conscience?
2. Why is not conscience a universal rule of action?
3. What inference is drawn relative to sin?
4. How is this illustrated?
5. What would make Mary feel guilty?
6. What is said of another little girl?
7. What makes the difference between them?
8. Are instances of perverted conscience common?
9. How does conscience become seared and deadened?
10. What was Frank's teacher in the habit of requiring?
11. For what did Frank turn back?
12. Whom did he meet on his way home?
13. What did his schoolmate ask Frank to do?
14. How did Frank feel when he heard that?
15. What did the boy do then?
16. What name did he sign to the note?
17. What was the crime then committed? (Forgery.)
18. What was Frank's first impulse?
19. What did he do?

20. What did his conscience tell him?
21. What will be the result if he obeys the voice of conscience?
22. What if he disobeys?

LESSON SEVENTH.

THE STORY OF FRANK CONCLUDED.

Frank had been an hour or more in school, and had recited his lesson in spelling before anything was said about his absence the day before. He began to think that the teacher had forgotten it, and would not ask for his excuse. He had almost made up his mind not to give in the note written by his schoolmate, and intended to promise his teacher to bring an excuse the next day.

He felt quite easy in his mind when he concluded to do this. This was the right way, and conscience told him so. But Frank had not really decided the matter. He thought he had, but he kept constantly thinking of the opposite course. He had never been caught without an excuse when one was called for. His mother would have given him one if he had asked for it. That he did not ask for it was owing entirely to forgetfulness on his part. It could make but little difference to the teacher who wrote the excuse, so long as he had been really detained by his parents.

Then, to be sure, there was the forgery of his mother's name; but Frank did not forge it, nor even ask any one to do it. He began to doubt whether any of the guilt of that act would fall to his share, even if he should hand in the note.

Revolving these and similar thoughts in his mind while attempting to do a sum in multiplication, suddenly the teacher cried out,

"Frank, did you bring an excuse for yesterday's absence?"

Without stopping to think, Frank answered "Y-e-s, sir," and stepping to the master's desk he laid down the note.

I can give you no idea of Frank's feelings when he returned to his seat and saw the forged excuse lying unopened on the desk of the teacher, who seemed to pay no attention to it, but continued the business he was engaged in, that of setting copies for the boys of the first class.

Surely, thought Frank, he knows all about

it; so do all the boys, or why do they keep staring at me so? The paper, dirty and crumpled, looked very different from the neatly written notes sent by the poor boy's mother. Every moment he expected to see the teacher take it up and expose him to the whole school. He did not know what punishment would ensue. The crime seemed dreadful, and the more he thought of it the worse it appeared. The sufferings of those few minutes amounted to agony, and he began to think the teacher would never finish writing copies.

And now Frank's troubled conscience seemed to whisper to him the only course proper to be taken. This was, as soon as an opportunity offered, to go to the teacher and confess his fault. "I will do it," said he to himself, "as soon as he stops writing."

He ought to have done it at once, and happy had it been for him if he had done so; but he waited for a better opportunity, which, alas! never came.

One duty after another required the teacher's attention, and it was within a few minutes of the time of dismissing school when, taking up the note, he hastily exclaimed, "Why, Frank, I never knew your mother write with a pencil before."

This was the time for confession, and Frank was almost, but not quite ready to make it. The teacher appeared to be satisisfied that the note was not a forgery. If he had doubted that, Frank would probably have confessed; but hearing what he said, all danger of being found out seemed to vanish away, and he remained silent.

Unfortunately for Frank, the trick was never discovered. His conscience became more and more callous. In a few months thereafter he palmed upon his teacher an excuse for absence, forged by himself, when he had really been playing truant; and soon he acquired the reputation of being a liar and the worst boy in the school.

Questions on Lesson VII.

1. What had Frank almost made up his mind to do?
2. How did he feel when he concluded to do this?
3. What did his conscience tell him?
4. But had Frank really decided the matter?
5. What was the subject of his thoughts?
6. State some of the reasons that passed through his mind.

7. What did he at length begin to doubt?
8. When the teacher asked if he had an excuse, what did Frank say?
9. Was that true?
10. How did Frank feel?
11. What troubled him?
12. What did conscience whisper?
13. Did he follow the dictates of his conscience?
14. What remark did the teacher make about the note?
15. Of what did he seem satisfied?
16. What was unfortunate for Frank?
17. What is said of his conscience afterward?
18. What did he do in a few months thereafter?
19. What reputation did he then acquire?

LESSON EIGHTH.

VIOLATIONS OF CONSCIENCE.

It is not possible to tell how bad a person may become who continues to violate his conscience. There is no limit to the depth of wickedness into which he may fall. Every admonition of conscience which he refuses to heed renders the next admonition weaker, and more likely to be disregarded. Thus proceeding, the time comes when conscience appears to be stupefied, if not dead. At first, to speak figuratively, she utters her remonstrances against comparatively trivial acts of wrong-doing with a voice like thunder. If unheeded she is less earnest in her next appeal, speaks more and more gently as offenses increase in number and in enormity, lowers her voice by degrees to a gentle whisper, and finally becomes utterly silent.

Sometimes you may hear profane language, cursing and swearing. A chill creeps over you, and you tremble as you listen to such horrible blasphemy.

Strange as it may seem, there was a time when he who now utters it so glibly would have felt, at hearing it from the lips of another, just as you now feel at hearing it from him. The boy's first oath faltered upon his lips, so did the second and the third. But he used that kind of language, regardless of the voice of conscience, until he could take God's name in vain without a shudder, and utter the most blasphemous language with boldness. Now conscience troubles him not, and he scarcely knows that his language is continually offensive to all right-minded persons.

There is a man now in the state prison

who will end his days there. He says that when he was a boy he was tempted to steal a dime from his mother. His conscience, of course, warned him against it. But he yielded to the temptation, and was not detected. Another opportunity soon occurred, and he took a larger sum. He proceeded from one act of dishonesty to another, until he was taken up, tried, and found guilty of the crime which has shut him out from the society of his fellow-men.

The latter wicked acts of that man's life gave him little uneasiness except the fear of being discovered; but he will never forget the desperate struggle he had with his conscience when he first pilfered from his mother, nor the agony of remorse that stolen dime caused him until he got rid of it.

I was looking over a new dictionary the other day. I met there with a word that was not in any of the dictionaries in use when I was a boy. It was the active transitive verb *To Burke.* Perhaps you never heard of it before. It means, to murder a person for the purpose of selling the dead body to the doctors for dissection. A man whose name was Burke had done this, not in one instance only, but, as he confessed before he was hung, he had killed fifteen different persons, and sold their bodies to the surgeons for a few shillings apiece. Hence that hitherto unheard of crime was called Burking, and a new word found its way into the dictionary. It will associate the crime with the name of the criminal forever.

Now this man was once a little boy, and had, as you have, a conscience. I do not suppose he had the advantages that you derive from parental instruction, and teachers, and kind friends. Still he had a conscience that used to trouble him when he was about to do wrong, just as yours sometimes troubles you. But he went on, step by step, from one act of wickedness to another, until at length he committed murder. This was so far beyond his other crimes that conscience awoke, and his remorse and agony were for a time almost unendurable. But he pursued his bloody career until, as he confessed himself, he had no more regard for the life of a man than a butcher has for that of a sheep. His conscience was utterly benumbed, and he expiated his guilt upon the gallows, a fearful example of the depth of wickedness into which he may fall who persistently violates the warnings and the admonitions of his conscience.

Questions on Lesson VIII.

1. What is said of one who continues to violate his conscience?
2. Into how great wickedness may such a one fall?
3. What results from disregarding the admonitions of conscience?
4. Continuing to do so, what follows?
5. What is said of the voice of conscience?
6. What about the blasphemer?
7. Relate what is said about a man in the state prison?
8. Did his former or latter wicked acts give him most uneasiness?
9. How is this to be accounted for?
10. What is that new word recently found in the dictionary?
11. What does it mean?
12. Has such a thing ever been done?
13. What is said of the man who was guilty of this crime?
14. When this man first committed murder how did he feel?
15. Continuing in his course how did he feel?
16. What became of him?

LESSON NINTH.

CONSCIENCE ENLIGHTENED AND QUICKENED.

CONSCIENCE, as we have seen, may be weakened; and its power to repel from wrong actions very much impaired, if not totally destroyed. So, too, its power to discriminate between right and wrong may be very greatly lessened. This, however, does not excuse the guilt, or in any degree interfere with the responsibility of those who thus injure, and weaken, and deaden their own consciences. On the contrary, their guilt increases just as fast as they do this, and no one's responsibility can be evaded by his own conduct. Every one sees, in a moment, that the actual guilt of the man Burke was none the less because his conscience had become utterly callous.

Conscience may be enlightened and educated. It may be quickened, and rendered more keen to discern the difference between right and wrong, and more clear-sighted to perceive always the path of duty.

One of the methods of improving the discriminating power of conscience is CAREFULLY TO HEED ITS DICTATES, AND RESOLUTELY TO ABSTAIN FROM DOING WHAT SEEMS TO BE FORBIDDEN BY IT. This is a very simple rule and easily remembered. It implies, however, and this introduces a second rule upon the subject, that we cultivate A HABIT OF CONSIDERING AND REFLECTING before we decide upon doing, or leaving undone, any particular action.

"Let us go a swimming," said one of a party of boys as they came out of school on a warm afternoon in summer.

"Agreed," "agreed," was the cry from all except Theodore, who was as fond of going into the water as any of them, and who was, in fact, the best swimmer of the party. Why did he hesitate? There was nothing wrong in the proposal in itself considered. But Theodore's mother had told him to come straight home as soon as school was out. She had not told him why, nor given any reason for the request; but he remembered it, and firmly said no to the urgent entreaties of his schoolmates.

What Theodore's mother wanted him for that afternoon is of no consequence. He found out when he reached home, and had

THEODORE AND HIS MOTHER.

far greater enjoyment in the thought that he did right in resisting the temptation than he could have had if, without stopping to reflect, he had shared in the fun of his companions.

So it is in all cases. You cannot remember doing a single thing in opposition to your conscience which was not a source of pain to you; nor can you think of one instance in which you obeyed its voice and had any cause to regret it.

TO STOP AT ONCE, AND IMMEDIATELY DECIDE THE QUESTION, IS IT RIGHT? is then the proper course for all who wish to act conscientiously and to educate conscience. If Theodore had hesitated and parleyed, if he had allowed himself to weigh in his mind the enjoyment proposed, and had taken into the account the fact that his mother did not speak *very* positively, and that he did not know why she wanted him to come straight home, it is very likely that he would have acted in opposition to his conscience, and thus have weakened its moral power instead of strengthening it.

But sometimes conscience is unable to decide positively with reference to any proposed course of action. You may pause and reflect, and the result is a doubt. What is to be done then?

That question is easily answered. Let us take the case of Patrick, of whom we spoke in the fifth lesson. He violated his conscience by eating meat on Friday, because he had been taught that it was wrong to eat it on that day. Suppose now that Patrick had been on a journey, and did not know whether it was Friday or Saturday when they set the beef-steak before him. If he had no opportunity of ascertaining, and was really in doubt, his course was clear, namely, to let the meat alone. There could be no harm in that. So, in all cases, do nothing of which you doubt the propriety.

Questions on Lesson IX.

1. What is said of the discriminating power of conscience?
2. May guilt be lessened as conscience becomes callous?
3. What about man's responsibility in such cases?
4. May conscience be enlightened or educated?
5. What is the first method mentioned for this object?
6. What is the second?

7. What proposition was made to a party of boys?
8. Did all the party agree to it?
9. Why did Theodore hesitate to go with them?
10. What was the result of his refusal to go with them?
11. What is said of similar actions?
12. What would probably have been the result if Theodore had hesitated?
13. What reasons for going might have occurred to him?
14. Can conscience in all cases decide promptly with reference to any course of action?
15. What will sometimes be the result?
16. What is to be done in such cases?

LESSON TENTH.

THE GREAT TEACHER.

We saw in a former lesson that it is not possible to set a limit to the depth of degradation into which they may fall who persistently violate conscience.

It is true also that conscience may be instructed and enlightened to an unlimited extent. By listening reverently to its voice, and by yielding to all its monitions, conscience becomes more and more susceptible of the boundary line between right and wrong, and more quick in forming its decisions with reference to any proposed course of action. So long as we have the power of thought and reflection we may continue to enlighten and instruct our consciences.

But it by no means follows that conscience can become an absolutely perfect guide. We may reach a point, in this respect, indefinitely near perfection; but no mortal may hope to claim that his is an unerring and absolutely perfect conscience.

There is fear too that in this process of educating conscience it may become over-scrupulous. A morbid or diseased conscience is a source of misery to its possessor and to all about him.

You have heard of those heathen whose moral sense had been educated to regard it as wicked to destroy animal life, and who, when shown by a microscope that the water they drank was full of minute living creatures, stood aghast with horror. They were troubled at the thought of what they had done in the past, and were more troubled as to what they should do in the future.

We say their conscientious scruples were absurd. But our saying that would not make the absurdity manifest to them, nor quiet the reproaches of conscience which charged them, however absurdly, with having done wrong.

From these two considerations, namely, that conscience may become unduly sensitive, and thus prove a source of continual uneasiness; and secondly, from the fact that we may not hope to educate conscience up to a state of unerring perfection, there arises the necessity of another standard of duty, something that shall not fluctuate with the opinions, nor the prejudices, nor even the varying education of the children of men. We feel the continual need of a teacher whose instructions shall be perfect, and from whose decisions there can be no appeal. And there is such a standard. There is such a teacher. Jesus Christ is the teacher, and the Bible, including the Old and the New Testaments, is the standard, or as we may reverently call it, HIS text-book. True, the Bible contains much that is merely historical, and a great deal of biography, the sayings and doings of bad as well as of good men, sacred songs, proverbs, and predictions of the future.

Many of these things may seem to have little bearing on the abstract question of morals, yet were they all *written for our learning.* Rom. xv, 4. And in addition there is ample instruction with reference to every question of moral duty.

It is true also that Jesus Christ is not distinctly revealed as actually present in his personal character in the narrative and other portions of the Old Testament. But his spirit pervades the whole. Things concerning him are found in the books of Moses, commonly called the Pentateuch; in the Psalms; in each of the prophets, and in short in every part of the Old Testament. Luke xxiv, 27 and 44, and Acts x, 43. The Bible is full of Christ from beginning to end, and his object therein is to teach us our duty to ourselves, to one another, and to our Maker. Hence, moral science, or ethics, having an absolutely perfect teacher, is a perfect science, free from discordant and clashing theories like those which have been put forth on other branches of knowledge.

Men may differ in opinion as to what Jesus really taught; but when they admit him to be a divine instructor they cannot honestly question the propriety and the duty of following his instructions when made clear to their understandings.

It will be found too, as we proceed, that in most instances the reason why men dispute about the moral questions settled by Jesus Christ, is not because of inability to understand, so much as on account of unwillingness to receive the simplicity, the purity, and the unbending strictness of the moral science which he taught.

Questions on Lesson X.

1. To what extent may conscience be instructed and enlightened?
2. Can conscience ever become a perfect guide?
3. What is meant by a morbid or diseased conscience?
4. Of what is such a conscience the source?
5. What is said of certain heathen?
6. What do we say of their conscientious scruples?
7. What effect would our saying that have on them?
8. What are the two considerations here mentioned?
9. What thence arises?
10. What must be the peculiarities of this new standard?
11. Of what do we feel the continual need?
12. What is this standard?
13. Who is this teacher?
14. What does the Bible contain?
15. Whose spirit pervades the Old Testament?
16. What are the books of Moses called?

17. Can you repeat those passages in the New Testament which teach that Christ is revealed in the Old?
18. What is the object of Christ in the Bible?
19. Christ being a perfect teacher, what follows?
20. Can the duty of following Christ's instructions be honestly questioned?

LESSON ELEVENTH.

INSUFFICIENCY OF THE LIGHT OF NATURE.

It has frequently been asserted that what is called the light of nature, taken in connection with conscience, is an all-sufficient guide to every moral duty. This is said by those who question the authenticity of the sacred Scriptures, or who deny the necessity of a divine revelation.

It is not to be denied that learned men have given to the world very plausible theories of moral science, in which the Bible has been carefully kept out of sight. So, too, treatises upon what is called *natural* theology have been framed, in which no notice has been taken of the fact that God has made a revelation of himself to the children of men. The existence of a Supreme Being, and the attributes or perfections of his character, have been logically proved, and our duty to him and to one another has been made plain, and all this has been done without any acknowledgment of indebtedness to the sacred Scriptures.

Let it ever be remembered, however, that the philosophers who have thus argued and reasoned were in possession of the Bible before they commenced their investigations. They did not, as they seem to pretend, *by searching find out God.* Job xi, 7. They did not, by the mere light of reason, evolve a pure system of morals. The system having been made known, it was not difficult to show its beauty and to prove its superiority. The existence and attributes of God being first revealed, it evinced no wonderful ingenuity to prove that existence and to establish those attributes. And this is all that natural theology has ever done.

In proof of this statement take the remarkable fact, that in all the teachings of these philosophers THEY HAVE NEVER YET SUCCEEDED IN MAKING KNOWN ONE SOLITARY

PERFECTION OF JEHOVAH WHICH WAS NOT PREVIOUSLY REVEALED IN THE BIBLE. There can be no doubt that he has other perfections—attributes of character which are utterly concealed from us in our present state. The Bible does not profess fully to reveal God. With all the light we derive from its pages we cannot *find him out to perfection.* Job xi, 7. We look in vain to natural theology to aid us in this search, and every body sees the absurdity of invoking the light of reason to dispel the thick darkness in which HE dwells.

Secondly, in all the teachings of natural religion, as it is called, there are made known to us NO MORAL DUTIES AS DUE FROM MAN TO HIS NEIGHBOR OR HIS MAKER, SAVE ONLY THOSE WHICH ARE TAUGHT IN THE SACRED SCRIPTURES. The specific duty being revealed, it is not difficult for human reason to show its propriety and its necessity; but it is a little too arrogant for human reason, after kindling its torch at the revelation given us by the Father of lights, to throw discredit upon that revelation, or to say that it was unnecessary.

The same truth is seen, thirdly, IN THE ABSURD THEORIES OF LEARNED MEN; WHO

HAD NOT THE LIGHT OF DIVINE REVELATION TO GUIDE THEM. Among the heathens of ancient Greece and Rome there were profound philosophers and acute logicians. Many of them brought all the powers of their mighty intellects to bear upon the question of man's duty and destiny. And what results did they reach? Some of them seem to have had an idea of beings superior to men. But whether there might be one God or ten thousand the wisest of them could not tell. Indeed, the latter seems to have been the prevailing sentiment, and was evidently most consonant with the teachings of unaided human reason. The most profoundly learned of the ancient heathen philosophers, Socrates, after teaching philosophy for many years, directed his attendants, just as he was bidding this world farewell, to sacrifice, on his behalf, a cock to an imaginary god called Esculapius. We smile at the absurdity; yet Socrates was a philosopher, an earnest student of natural theology, a man who, if he had lived in our day, with the light that we have streaming from the sacred page, would have filled both hemispheres with his renown.

The same course of argument leads to the conclusion that the duties we owe to one another, although clearly perceived when once made known, and susceptible of demonstration when revealed, are nevertheless, in the first instance, to be derived from that *word* which, in the language of the psalmist, is a *lamp unto our feet, and a light unto our path.* Psalm cxix, 105.

Questions on Lesson XI.

1. What is frequently asserted?
2. Who say this?
3. What have learned men given to the world?
4. What is said of treatises on natural theology?
5. Of what were these philosophers in possession?
6. What is said to be all that natural theology has done?
7. What is the first argument in proof of that statement?
8. Is it probable that God has other attributes besides those revealed in the Bible?
9. What argument is next adduced?
10. What is said to be a little too arrogant?
11. What argument is next set forth?
12. Among whom were profound philosophers?
13. Upon what did they exercise their reasoning powers?

14. Were they able to prove the existence of a supreme being?
15. As to the number of gods, what was the prevailing sentiment?
16. Who was Socrates?
17. What did he direct his attendants to do just before his death?
18. What is said would have been his celebrity if he had lived in our day?
19. To what other conclusion does this course of argument conduct?
20. What does the psalmist call the word of God?

LESSON TWELFTH.

HARMONY OF THE OLD AND THE NEW TESTAMENTS.

It is said in the sixth Article of Religion, as found in the Discipline of the Church, that the Old Testament is not contradictory to the New. We may go further, and say that not only are they not contradictory, but that they are both one, one in design, one in doctrine, one in precept. What is taught in the New Testament is taught also in the Old; with this difference, that things dimly shadowed forth in the law, in the

Psalms, and in the prophets, are in the Gospels, the Acts, and the Epistles made clear and distinct. *Think not*, said Jesus, *that I am come to destroy the law or the prophets: I am not come to destroy, but to fulfill.* Matt. v, 17.

A few illustrations of this truth may, with propriety, be considered before we enter upon the ethical teachings of the Bible.

Let us take, as our first illustration, those cardinal doctrines which some suppose to be taught only in the New Testament, repentance, faith, holiness. Jesus Christ and the apostles preached the duty of repentance, and urged it upon their hearers. And what is repentance but a practical exemplification of the duty enjoined by the prophet, *Cease to do evil, learn to do well.* Isa. i, 16, 17. Is pardon promised to the penitent in the Gospel? Even so it is written in the Old Testament, *Whoso confesseth and forsaketh his sins shall have mercy.* Prov. xxviii, 13.

The great doctrine of justification by faith runs all through both Testaments. It is exemplified away back in the book of Genesis, (xv, 6,) where it is said of Abram, before his name was changed, *He believed in the Lord, and it was counted to him for righteousness.* The glorious truth which set on fire the soul of Luther, and ushered in the Reformation, was not first proclaimed by Paul. You will find the very words, *The just shall live by his faith*, in one of the minor prophets. Hab. ii, 4.

Without holiness no man shall see the Lord (Heb. xii, 14) is thought by many to be a peculiarity of apostolic teaching. It is but the echo of the injunction running all through the Levitical law, *Be ye holy, for I am the Lord your God.* Lev. xx, 7.

So too with the precepts of the Bible. To the moral law, as found in the Ten Commandments, Jesus makes no addition. He explains and enforces, but adds nothing. The Psalmist had said, *The law of the Lord is perfect.* Psa. xix, 7. Jesus and the apostles attest the same truth. Nothing is added to it. Nothing may be taken from it. *Till heaven and earth pass, one jot or one tittle shall in no wise pass from the law till all be fulfilled.* Matt. v, 18.

The Jews, in the time of the Saviour, had incorporated with the law which requires us to love our neighbor the monstrous addition that we should hate our enemy. That clause is not found in the Bible. On the contrary, the spirit of the Old Testament is in harmony with the teachings of Jesus: *Love your enemies.* Matt. v, 44.

With great clearness the New Testament teaches the doctrine of a final day of reckoning, the everlasting rewards of the righteous, and the endless misery of the wicked. In the Old Testament the same great facts are revealed, if not with as much clearness with equal solemnity and certainty. A thousand years before Christ unfolded visions of the great day of judgment, with its dread decisions, Solomon had said, *God shall bring every work into judgment, with every secret thing, whether it be good or whether it be evil.* Eccl. xii, 14.

The happiness of heaven is beautifully dwelt upon by the Saviour and his apostles. So it was by the psalmist and the prophets.

In thy presence, says David, *is fullness of joy; at thy right hand are pleasures forevermore.* Psa. xvi, 11. In all the declarations of the New Testament with reference to the doom of the finally impenitent, there is nothing more fearful than the words of the psalmist: *The wicked shall be turned into hell and all the nations that forget God.* Psa. ix, 17. And again: *Upon the wicked he shall rain snares, fire and brimstone, and a horrible tempest: this shall be the portion of their cup.* Psa xi, 6.

Questions on Lesson XII.

1. Repeat the sixth article of religion as found in the Discipline.
2. In what sense are the Old and New Testaments one?
3. What difference do you find in their teachings?
4. What does Jesus Christ say of the object of his coming?
5. What are called the cardinal doctrines of the New Testament?
6. Where is repentance inculcated in the Old Testament?
7. Repeat the promise made in the Old Testament to the penitent.
8. In which book of the Bible is justification by faith first taught?
9. What is said of Abram?
10. Repeat the declaration made by the prophet Habakkuk.
11. Where in the Old Testament is the doctrine of holiness taught?
12. What is here said of the moral law?

13. What does the psalmist say of it?
14. And what is the declaration of Jesus Christ?
15. What addition had the Jews made to the moral law?
16. With what does the spirit of the Old Testament harmonize?
17. Is a day of final reckoning taught in the Old Testament?
18. Quote the passage.
19. How long before the advent of Christ was that written?
20. Quote a passage from the Psalms relative to the happiness of heaven.
21. Repeat the two passages which speak of the doom of the wicked.

LESSON THIRTEENTH.

QUARTERLY REVIEW OF THE PRECEDING STUDIES.

THE questions now to be asked are founded upon the studies of the last three months. Answers, for the most part, may be gathered from the lessons; although some of the questions will require the exercise of the student's reasoning faculties, and the assistance of the teacher may be necessary in a few instances.

1. What is the general subject that you have been studying?
2. What facts have been taken for granted in pursuing this study?
3. How do we know that there is a God?
4. What do you understand by rational creatures?
5. What is reason?
6. Can you distinguish between reason and instinct?
7. What contradicts the statement that twice two are five?
8. What is a hexagon?
9. What do you understand by the moral sense?
10. Why are not dumb animals capable of moral actions?
11. What is to be considered when judging of a moral action?
12. Can you repeat the story of Charlie and the broken pane of glass?
13. Frederic also broke a window: how was it done?
14. In the various methods of doing wrong, on what does the degree of blame depend?
15. Why should we be very jealous of the

motives by which we profess to be governed?

16. Will a good intention justify an act that is wrong in itself?
17. State the supposed case of a boy who played truant.
18. Relate the incident of the rum-seller and the ladies.
19. What inferences are drawn from that incident?
20. Relate the story of the doctor and the sick man.
21. How far is conscience a safe rule of conduct?
22. Can you illustrate the fact that he who violates his conscience does wrong?
23. What is it always safe not to do?
24. Can you give an instance of the guilt of falsehood being incurred when the truth was told?
25. Relate the history of St. Paul so far as relates to his course of conduct as a persecutor.
26. Why may not conscience be a universal rule of action?
27. Give some illustrations of the fact that what is sin in one is not always sin in another.

28. Give in your own language the story of Frank.
29. What ought Frank to have done with the forged note?
30. How did Frank feel as the note lay on the teacher's desk?
31. What made him think that all the boys were staring at him?
32. What is the effect of every unheeded admonition of conscience?
33. Relate the case of the boy who stole a dime from his mother.
34. What new word was derived from a great crime?
35. By what means may conscience be educated and quickened?
36. How is the discriminating power of conscience weakened?
37. What is said about Theodore and his schoolmates?
38. What should be our course of conduct when we have doubts of the propriety of any action?
39. To what extent may conscience be instructed or enlightened?
40. Does it thence follow that conscience may become an all-sufficient guide in all cases?

41. Can you illustrate a morbid or diseased conscience?
42. What is said of the ancient heathen philosophers?
43. What is the great text-book of moral science?
44. By what arguments are shown the insufficiency of what is called natural theology?
45. Give some illustrations of the harmony between the Old and the New Testaments.
46. State allusions to Christ that are found in the Old Testament.
47. Quote some passages from the Old Testament which have reference to faith, to repentance, to holiness.
48. Where in the Old Testament are we taught that there will be a day of judgment?
49. What are the scriptural proofs of the happiness of heaven?
50. What is said in the Old Testament of the future punishment of the wicked?
51. Can you quote other passages from the Old Testament in proof of doctrines taught by Jesus Christ?

LESSON FOURTEENTH.

CLASSIFICATION OF MORAL DUTIES.

THE various moral duties may be classified in three divisions. The first includes the duties we owe to ourselves, the second those we owe to our fellow-creatures, and the third our duties to our Creator.

This division is made merely for convenience and for the assistance of memory. It is not possible to transgress in the one class without in a greater or less degree offending in the others. If I neglect any duty to myself or to my neighbor, I offend God, whose will is the foundation of all moral obligation.

So, too, I cannot wrong a fellow-creature without injuring myself; and there are very few persons so utterly friendless and solitary that they can neglect duties which they owe to themselves without doing wrong to associates and relatives, for *We are every one members, one of another*, (Rom. xii, 5,) and *None of us liveth to himself*. Rom. xiv, 7.

A great mistake is made by those teachers of Christian morality who denounce *self-*

love as altogether wrong. The error arises from confounding two things that are essentially distinct, to wit, self-love and selfishness. The latter is indeed hateful and forbidden. The former is a natural instinct of every living creature, and one that specially distinguishes the human race. The Great Teacher constantly appeals to it. He makes every one's self-love the standard by which to measure duty to a fellow-creature. His command is, (Matt. v, 43,) *Thou shalt love thy neighbor as thyself;* and the frequency with which this fundamental principle is stated in the New Testament is worthy of note. It is repeated in Matt. xix, 19, and xxii, 39; in the parallel passages in Mark (xii, 31) and Luke (x, 27.) It is reiterated by Saint Paul in the Epistle to the Romans (xiii, 9,) and in the Epistle to the Galatians (v, 14.) Saint James quotes it also, and calls it the royal law, (ii, 8.) *As* we love ourselves is thus declared to be the royal, that is, the heaven-ordained standard by which to measure our love to others. If then I do not love myself at all; if, in other words, I have no self-love, I am thereby excused from loving my neighbor, an absurdity that needs no refutation.

At the same time this command sets a limit beyond which I may not pass in my love of self, and if it were universally obeyed it would utterly destroy all selfishness. How could any one be selfish, or love himself inordinately, if he really loved others in the same degree?

Self-love is the basis of the first class of moral duties, that is, of the duties which we owe to ourselves; and these we now propose to consider, first, as referring to the body; secondly, to the intellect; and thirdly, to the soul.

A human body is one of the most wonderful of the works of God. It is a specimen of HIS handiwork, admirably fitted for the purposes for which he made it. It is not, as some tell us, merely a dwelling-place for the soul, confining it to the earth, and interfering with its upward aspirations. It is an integral portion of the individual. If we may say, The body is not the man, so also we may say with equal truth, The soul is not the man, and the spirit is not the man. It is the union of the three that makes the individual. Hence the expressive language of the apostle: *I pray God your whole spirit, and soul, and body be preserved blameless unto the coming of our Lord Jesus Christ.* 1 Thes. v, 23.

A few additional passages may serve to correct some crude and unworthy notions relative to the human body. You are directed to glorify God in your body as well as in your spirit; and for so doing you have this wondrous but all-sufficient reason, *your body is the temple of the Holy Ghost.* 1 Cor. vi, 19, 20.

It is expressly said, too, (1 Cor. vi, 18,) that the body may be sinned against; and the apostle, speaking of himself, says: *I keep under my body, and bring it into subjection, lest that by any means, when I have preached to others, I myself should be a castaway.* 1 Cor. ix, 27.

Questions on Lesson XIV.

1. Into how many divisions are moral duties divided?
2. What are they?
3. For what purpose is this division made?
4. What is said to be impossible?
5. What is the foundation of moral obligation?
6. When we wrong a fellow-creature what else do we do?

7. Repeat the passages quoted from the Epistle to the Romans.
8. What is said to be a great mistake?
9. Whence does the error arise?
10. What is said of selfishness?
11. What of self-love?
12. What is the standard by which we are to measure love to our neighbors?
13. In how many places is this principle stated in the New Testament?
14. What absurdity is here alluded to?
15. What would destroy all selfishness?
16. What is the basis of the first class of moral duties?
17. What duties are included in the first class?
18. How are these subdivided?
19. What is said of the human body?
20. Repeat the passage from First Thessalonians.
21. What do we learn from that?
22. What is said of the body in 1 Cor. vi, 19, 20?
23. What by the apostle in the same epistle, ix, 27?

LESSON FIFTEENTH.

CLEANLINESS.

Cleanliness, said the learned Jeremy Taylor, is next to godliness. Whether we adopt the sentiment literally or not, we do not hesitate to give personal cleanliness the first place among the duties which we owe to ourselves. You have heard little children cry when the nurse undertook to wash them. I have known larger boys and girls, when they have been taught to wash themselves, do it unwillingly and imperfectly. For our own sakes, and for the sake of those with whom we associate, the duty of personal cleanliness is one that ought to be scrupulously attended to: for our own sakes, because it conduces to health; and for the sake of others, because its neglect is always offensive.

The application of a little water to the face and hands once a day is very far from being all that is required. The teeth, the hair, the finger-nails deserve attention quite as much as the face; and the entire body ought frequently to be washed in clean water. All this is self-evident; and it is hardly worth while for a boy or girl who is not convinced of the necessity of personal cleanliness to go any further in the study of the moral duties which we owe to ourselves and to one another.

It is necessary here to notice certain unclean habits into which the young are sometimes led by evil example. I wish it was not necessary to say anything on the subject; but I remember a little blue-eyed boy, with flaxen hair, who was a scholar in the first Sunday-school class that I ever taught. He was about ten years old, and his name was Felix. One day he went home from school, and, without saying a word to anybody in the house, threw himself upon his bed. He was very sick. His mother came into his room as soon as she returned from church, and was much surprised to find him there. He began to vomit, and the doctor was sent for. He suspected the cause; and Felix, on being questioned, admitted that he had been trying to smoke a cigar. One of the larger scholars, a bad boy, who afterward went to sea and was drowned, had coaxed him to do it.

Felix recovered in a few days, and you would have thought he would never try again to smoke. But he did, and kept on trying until he could not only smoke without being made sick, but began to think that he could not do without a cigar.

As is always the case with bad habits when indulged, one led to another. Soon he began to chew tobacco, and then to persuade other boys to do so. I asked th superintendent to put him in another class, as I had tried in vain to break him of his bad habits.

I suppose we ought to try to teach such boys; but I think it would be well to put them in a class by themselves where they would not be likely to corrupt others by their example.

Only think how it would sound in a Sunday-school to hear one class called the smokers or the tobacco chewers, or to include in one all of any unclean habits. Who would like to be a member of "*the dirty class?*"

Not quite so bad as chewing tobacco, but very likely to lead to it, is the habit some boys indulge in of chewing gum or shoemaker's wax. Girls, too, sometimes fall into this practice, and I knew one who was hardly ever seen except at meal-times without a piece of India rubber in her mouth. It was a fortunate thing for her that one night she awoke in great distress, almost choked to death. She had gone to bed with a large piece of India rubber in her mouth, which in her sleep she swallowed. By masticating it constantly for several days, in the mean time swallowing the dirty saliva, it had become quite soft. A physician happened to be close at hand, and by his skill it was extracted. Thus, in all probability, she escaped death by strangling, and was effectually cured of that bad and uncleanly habit.

Questions on Lesson XV.

1. What was Jeremy Taylor's remark about cleanliness?
2. To what place is personal cleanliness entitled among the duties we owe to ourselves?
3. How do some boys and girls wash themselves?
4. To what does personal cleanliness conduce?
5. What is always offensive?
6. Is it enough to wash the hands and face once a day?
7. What else ought to be done?
8. Is argument on this subject necessary?
9. What is said of those who are not convinced of the necessity of cleanliness?
10. What was the name of the little boy here spoken of?
11. Why did he go home from school?
12. What made him sick?
13. How was he induced to smoke?
14. Did his sickness cure him of the habit?
15. What followed?
16. What suggestion is made as to scholars of dirty habits?

17. What other bad habit is mentioned?
18. What is related of a little girl?
19. How did she escape strangling?
20. What effect was produced?

LESSON SIXTEENTH.

IDLENESS, INDUSTRY, RECREATION.

THE teachings of the Bible are confirmed by the observations of experience, that there is no sin against the body more injurious than idleness. To have something to do, and to do it, seem to be the essential conditions of health and the law of physical development. It is a mistake to suppose that labor is a part of the original curse entailed upon our race in consequence of the first transgression. In the garden of Eden, before sin entered the world, the Lord gave to man directions to dress and to keep it. Gen. ii, 15. Afterward, indeed, when Adam was banished from the garden, the earth was cursed for his sake, and brought forth thorns and thistles, (Gen. iii, 18,) rendering its cultivation more difficult and precarious;

THE IDLER.

but the conformation of the human frame, with its mysterious union of body, soul, and spirit, evinces the original design of the Creator to have been that man's faculties should be brought into exercise, and that labor, mental or bodily, or both, is essential to his well-being. The commandment which enjoined rest on the Sabbath is equally explicit with reference to industry on the other days of the week. *Six days shalt thou labor and do all thy work.* Exod. xx, 9. Of the virtuous woman, whose price is far above rubies, the wise man says in her special commendation: *She looketh well to the ways of her household, and eateth not the bread of idleness.* Prov. xxxi, 27. The apostle Paul, who was himself one of the most industrious of men, beseeches those to whom he wrote (1 Thess. iv, 11) *to do their own business; and to work*, says he, *with your own hands, as we commanded you.* In his second epistle to the same people he is still more emphatic on the subject. He says: *When we were with you, this we commanded you, that if any would not work, neither should he eat.* 2 Thess. iii, 10.

It must be remembered that industry is not confined entirely to the work of the hands nor to bodily labor. Paul was not less industrious when he was writing his epistles to the different Churches, than when, at Corinth, he worked at his trade of tent making. Acts xviii, 3. Indeed, mental labor is often more fatiguing than what is usually called hard work, and is sometimes more important. A farmer, after a severe day's toil of plowing, met with a thin, pale-faced man taking a walk, who entered into conversation with him. They both complained of being very much fatigued, but the farmer, who had been at work in the field under a hot sun all day, was at a loss to conceive what could have fatigued the man who had done nothing but sit in a cool room poring over his books and papers. To him it seemed as if the student's life must be very easy, and of little use to the world. He altered his opinion, however, when he was told that the plow which he had been using was the invention of his companion, who had devoted days and nights to scientific investigations, and was at this time engaged in writing a book by which he expected to lighten the toil and increase the rewards of the husbandman.

It is very foolish in girls or boys to complain of hard lessons. Even if it could be done, it would not be wise to make all study easy. There is nothing so invigorating as persevering industry in the acquisition of knowledge, and nothing more satisfactory than the attainment of a really difficult lesson.

Rest after toil, and recreation after study

and confinement, are also essential to our well-being. But no one can rest unless he is weary, and the very word recreation implies that there has been a previons season of mental or bodily fatigue. I heard of a boy, indeed, who, when asked what occupation he intended to pursue when he became a man replied, "I think I'll be a retired gentleman." His answer was about as sensible as that of the clown, who, when asked what he would do if he had as much money as he wanted, replied, "I'd swing all day on a gate and eat fat bacon."

Questions on Lesson XVI.

1. What is here said of idleness?
2. What seems to be the essential condition of health?
3. What is said to be a mistake?
4. What direction was given to Adam and Eve?
5. When was the earth cursed?
6. How is the original design of the Creator manifested?
7. What is enjoined by the first clause of the fourth commandment?
8. Whose price is far above rubies?
9. What is said in her commendation?

10. Who is called one of the most industrious of men?
11. What does he enjoin upon the Thessalonians in his first epistle?
12. What does he say on that subject in the second epistle?
13. To what is not industry entirely confined?
14. What is said of Paul to illustrate that sentiment?
15. What is then said of mental labor?
16. Can you relate the illustration there given?
17. Is it wise to complain of hard lessons?
18. Why would it not be wise to make all study easy?
19. What are also said to be essential to our well-being?
20. What is necessary before we can rest?
21. What does recreation imply?

LESSON SEVENTEENTH.

RECREATION AND AMUSEMENTS.

Occasional recreation and amusement, we have said, are essential to health of body and to the continuance of mental vigor. There are, however, diversities of opinion as to what may be deemed appropriate relaxation for those who make the revealed will of God their standard.

One of the General Rules of the Church

forbids "the taking such diversions as cannot be used in the name of the Lord Jesus." This precludes (1.) ALL GAMES OF CHANCE. Cards, dice, and dominoes are of this character, all of which have in them the essential element that is called chance, and it is evident that the blessing of the Lord Jesus cannot be invoked upon them.

It is true, indeed, that there are those who, while they denounce games of chance when played for money, see nothing wrong in such games for mere amusement. But it is not easy to answer the question, "Why should an hour or two spent at the card-table *gratis* be consistent with virtue, and that same time spent in the same employment be condemned as criminal if it profits one's purse?"

(2.) There are precluded all those amusements which TEND TO EXCITE IMPURE THOUGHTS, such as dancing and theatrical entertainments. A clergyman being at a public house was urged to attend a ball. The company were all assembled, and the music was about to commence, when, stepping into the circle, he invited all to kneel down with him and unite in prayer for a blessing upon the amusement. Those present saw the incongruity, just as those who attend the theater would see it should the proposition be made to introduce their evening's entertainment in the same way.

(3.) Those amusements which INFLICT PAIN ON ANY LIVING CREATURE are of course to be avoided. It is surprising that any person should need to be reminded that we have no right to torture any of the animal creation. They derived their existence from the same God who gave us being, and are the subjects of his continual regard. Bull-baiting, cock-fighting, and kindred sports are confined for the most part to the uneducated, and are condemned by those who do not scruple to wound and mangle little birds in mere wantonness, to force that noble animal, the horse, to his utmost speed; and to seek gratification from pursuits quite as unworthy of an accountable human being as those which are condemned as low and vulgar.

(4.) Frequently THE OBJECT IN VIEW renders the amusement itself inexpedient and improper. There is nothing wrong in a foot-race between two boys; but if they make a wager on the issue, and if the one strives to outrun the other for the sake of winning the bet, it is evident that they do wrong. Their amusement partakes of the nature of gambling, which no circumstances can justify. There are many games the very essence of which seems to consist in winning and losing, and which ought always to be avoided. The principle is the same whether the stake be money or marbles, buttons or pins.

(5.) So also some amusements, not sinful in themselves, are to be shunned because of THE ASSOCIATIONS CONNECTED WITH THEM. A game of quoits might be beneficial exercise, conducive to health as well as relaxation; but if it could only be indulged on the premises of a liquor shop, and in the company of those who frequent such places for purposes of dram-drinking and merry-making, it were better to dispense with it altogether. The scriptural injunction, *Abstain from all appearance of evil,* (1 Thess. v, 22,) is a rule always applicable in such cases.

(6.) It is a dictate equally of common sense and of sound morality, that amusements and recreation are to be indulged in WITH MODERATION. They are not to be made the business of life, nor to encroach upon the hours that ought to be devoted to study and labor. There is a time for all things, says the wise man, and he who devotes to amusement the hours which ought to be employed in the active duties of life, not only wrongs himself but is an injury to his associates.

Questions on Lesson XVII.

1. What are essential to health of body and mind?
2. On what subject is it said there are diversities of opinion?
3. What general rule of the Church is here quoted?
4. What are precluded by this rule?
5. What games of chance are specially named?
6. Why are they forbidden?
7. What question is hard to answer?
8. What other kinds of amusement are precluded by this rule?
9. What is said of a minister at a ball?
10. What effect did his invitation produce?
11. What would be the probable result of a similar invitation at a theater?
12. What is the third class of amusements that are forbidden?
13. Has man a right to torture any of the animal creation?
14. Mention some of the sports in which this law is violated.
15. What is the fourth class of improper amusements?
16. How is this illustrated?

17. What is gambling?
18. For what reason are amusements not sinful to be shunned?
19. Illustrate this.
20. What Scripture is quoted?
21. What is the last general remark on the subject?

LESSON EIGHTEENTH.

TEMPERANCE—MODERATION—CHASTITY.

By temperance we understand habitual moderation in the indulgence of the appetites and passions. The word is thus seen to be of extensive signification. Of course those err who confine their ideas of temperance merely to the use of intoxicating liquor.

Drunkenness is indeed a grievous offense not only against the body, but the soul, and the teachings of the Bible are pointed and severe in its denunciation. If you will read that passage of Scripture wherein those who are given to this vice are forewarned as to their future destiny, you will be startled not only at the declaration itself, but at the terrible catalogue of crimes with which drunkenness is associated. Perhaps you can commit to memory those two verses, the ninth and tenth of the sixth chapter of the First Epistle to the Corinthians. If you do they will have a tendency to restrain you from taking the first step in the way that leads to so dreadful a result. And the avoidance of the first step is the only security you can have against taking a second and a third, the only safeguard against the insidious power of an appetite which had no relish for strong drink until depraved and corrupted by indulgence. Total abstinence from all intoxicating drinks, while it never did and never can do injury to any one, is always a guaranty of safety.

But temperance has reference to eating as well as to drinking. Gluttony is forbidden as well as drunkenness, and is equally a wrong to the body. It is not so perceptible nor so rapid in its effects, but it is perhaps even more common, especially among the young. It is a very frequent cause of sickness; and death has been caused by eating too much far more frequently than by eating too little. The principle of self-love with which our Creator has endowed us, to say nothing of his will as revealed in the

Scriptures, not only forbids us to commit suicide by suddenly putting an end to life, but with equal clearness forbids us to do anything by which the wonderful mechanism of the body may be deranged and health destroyed or injured.

Temperance in the use of all our faculties, or, as it may more properly be called in this connection, moderation, is a dictate alike of the Bible and of reason. *Let your moderation be known unto all men* is the explicit injunction of the apostle. Phil. iv, 5. The world is full of examples of the evil consequences resulting from the immoderate pursuit of things in themselves desirable and even laudable. Among the educated men of the age a large proportion are invalids. Dyspepsia, liver complaints, derangement of the nervous system, and a host of other diseases, are at once the evidences and the penalty of the immoderate or intemperate pursuit of knowledge.

To the student these examples ought to be constant warnings against overtasking the brain, and against all the allurements of ambition to excel in the attainment of knowledge. It would be better not to be head of the class than to pay for reaching that eminence by an after lifetime of bodily suffering and a premature grave.

But caution is needed in the opposite direction. Perhaps more are immoderate in their amusements than in their studies. Some are so fond of play that they seem never to have enough. Others engage in any kind of game with such earnestness as to produce precisely the same effect as would too severe and too long-continued bodily labor. He or she who spends an undue proportion of time in play, or who pursues sport with too much eagerness, enervates and weakens the body, to say nothing of the injury thereby inflicted upon the mental powers.

Chastity is a duty most emphatically enjoined both in the Old and in the New Testaments. Nothing is more offensive in the sight of God, and nothing is more injurious to body and soul than the violation of this duty. The admonition of the apostle, *Keep thyself pure*, (1 Tim. v, 22,) may be regarded as the voice of God to all his intelligent creatures.

Questions on Lesson XVIII.

1. How do you define temperance?
2. What error on this subject is mentioned?
3. What is said of drunkenness?
4. Repeat 1 Cor. vi, 9, 10.
5. What is the only security against this vice?
6. What is said of gluttony?
7. How is it compared with drunkenness?
8. Of what is drunkenness a frequent cause?
9. What is said to have been caused by eating too much?
10. What is said of suicide?
11. How do you define *moderation?*
12. Of what is it the dictate?
13. What says the apostle in Philippians iv, 5?
14. Of what is the world said to be full?
15. What is the condition of a large portion of educated men?
16. What effect should these things have on the student?
17. What is said about being head of the class?
18. What is said of amusements?
19. What effect is produced by too earnest play?
20. Where is chastity emphatically enjoined?
21. What is said of its violation?
22. What is the admonition of the apostle?

LESSON NINETEENTH.

CONTENTMENT.

It is said of a certain eccentric rich man, that over the entrance to one of his estates he affixed a large placard containing these words: "This farm will be given to any one who is perfectly contented with his lot in life." In a little while an applicant made his appearance. "Are you perfectly contented?" asked the owner of the property. "I am," was the immediate reply. "Then," said the rich man, "go about your business. If you are perfectly contented you cannot want my farm."

This little anecdote, whether the fact ever occurred or not, illustrates a very common propensity of the human mind. It is a feeling of discontent with our lot in life, resulting in a covetous desire for the possessions of others. This feeling is always, to a greater or less extent, a source of unhappiness. It is specially forbidden in the tenth commandment, and its opposite is enjoined as a duty in various parts of the sacred Scriptures. *Thou shalt not covet*

(Exod. xx, 17) is a prohibition as imperative as Thou shalt not steal, and equally forbidden by the divine law, although human legislation takes no notice of it. *Let your conversation*, says the apostle, that is, your whole course of conduct, *be without covetousness, and be content with such things as ye have.* Heb. xiii, 5. *I have learned*, says he, *in whatever state I am, therewith to be content.* Phil. iv, 11. In this language he does not refer to his mental attainments, nor to his progress in the divine life. In both these respects he was continually anxious to make advances, to grow in grace and in knowledge. As is evident from the next verse, the apostle is speaking of his temporal affairs. The lesson he would impress on others he had himself acquired, and possibly a few suggestions may assist us in acquiring it.

And first, we all know that TO MURMUR AT OUR LOT IS OF NO USE. We may complain, and fret, and make ourselves and all who associate with us unhappy, but we cannot thereby alter our present circumstances or our prospects for the future. On the contrary, the more we yield to a murmuring spirit of discontent, the more discontented we become, and the more miserable.

2. It is well, occasionally at least, TO TURN OUR THOUGHTS FROM THOSE WHO ARE MORE PROSPEROUS THAN OURSELVES TO THE MULTITUDE AROUND US WHO ARE MORE UNFORTUNATE AND LESS SUCCESSFUL. You need not look far to find those whose lot you cannot envy. The poor, the sick, the afflicted, the bereaved are everywhere. A visit to the abodes of the suffering, if it does not cure a discontented mind, will have a tendency to make it thoroughly ashamed of itself, as was the case with little Lucy, who went with her mother one day to a lunatic asylum. There she saw and heard what she will never forget, and what, whenever she thinks of it, causes a feeling of thankfulness, that although she and her mother live in a little cottage, and have very few of the luxuries of life, they have their reason and a good degree of health, and a great many comforts of which others are utterly deprived.

3. Let us remember that while we may know the extent of our own troubles, MANY OF THOSE OF OUR FELLOW-CREATURES ARE ENTIRELY HIDDEN FROM US. He whose lot we envy is perhaps one of the most miserable of men.

It is related of an extremely wealthy

merchant, that his digestive organs were so impaired that he could only eat at a meal an exceedingly small portion of the coarsest food. He had a pair of scales upon his table, with which he weighed his ounce of dry biscuit for dinner. This he was in the habit of moistening with a little water-gruel; and if at any time he exceeded his allowance, great bodily suffering was the consequence. He was a very rich man; but the poorest street scavenger, who by the sweat of his face earned his daily food, of which he partook with a good appetite, would not have changed places with him.

4. It is well for you, when discontented with your lot, to endeavor properly TO ESTIMATE YOUR OWN DESERTS, and to contrast what you are with what you might have been. You might have been born blind, or deaf, or dumb, or all these combined; your lot might have been one of unceasing pain and suffering. With very little aid from the imagination you can realize that your condition might have been infinitely worse than it is. And can you persuade yourself that you *deserve* even the least of the blessings which you enjoy? You know you do not. You know that if you had your deserts all things that

make life desirable would be taken from you; for in all the circle of your acquaintance you cannot find an individual of whose heart you may safely say, It is more ungrateful than mine has been. No human being this side of the caverns of despair has any right to murmur or complain; but every one may find in the dispensations of God's providence abundant reason for thankfulness.

5. And finally, thus to see and acknowledge the hand of infinite wisdom and goodness in all the affairs of life cannot fail to check every discontented murmur, to banish every covetous desire, and to call forth that petition in the prayer taught us by the Saviour, *Thy will be done!*

Questions on Lesson XIX.

1. What is the subject of this lesson?
2. With what anecdote is it introduced?
3. What does the story illustrate?
4. What is usually the result of discontent?
5. Of what is that feeling always a source?
6. In which of the commandments is covetousness forbidden?
7. Can you repeat that commandment?
8. What is said on the subject in Hebrews xiii, 5?
9. What in Philippians iv, 11?

10. To what does the apostle here refer?
11. What is the first suggestion on the subject?
12. What is recommended in the second place?
13. Whom need we not look far to find?
14. Tell me about little Lucy and her mother?
15. What is the third thing to be remembered?
16. What may be the true condition of those we envy?
17. Relate what is said of a very rich man?
18. What is next recommended?
19. What might you have been?
20. What would you be if you had your deserts?
21. What is finally recommended?
22. What will result from such acknowledgment?

LESSON TWENTIETH.

CULTIVATION OF THE INTELLECT.

WE come now to consider, as a duty we owe to ourselves, the cultivation of the intellectual powers. It is with them in many respects as it is with the functions of the body. In the first place, it is not possible that in the present life either should reach a state of such perfection as to render further improvement impossible. Even by the most sedulous attention to the laws of health and the due exercise of all its powers, it is not to be supposed that the body will ever reach the state of perfection which that of Adam exhibited when it came from the hands of its Maker. At the same time it must be admitted that we may approach indefinitely near that state, and that in proportion as we approach it we increase our capacity of enjoyment and fulfill the design of our Creator.

The same may be said of the *mental faculties.* It is not in our power to set limits to the acquisition of knowledge of which the human mind is capable even in the present life. Wonderful and mysterious as is the human body, there is more of the Creator's glory revealed in the study of the mind. As we cannot tell to what perfection the former may attain, so much less can we conceive the extent of knowledge that the human mind is capable of receiving. Nobody supposes it to be impossible for man to go beyond the attainments yet made. We can easily imagine some future Newton to cast into the shade the researches and discoveries of that eminent philosopher. While then it is a duty to regard the laws of health so far as the body is concerned, much more imperative is the obligation to cultivate the intellect. Common sense and the Bible both refute the absurd and wicked notion that knowledge is incompatible with religion. The capabilities received from the Creator attest the fact that they must have been imparted for purposes of improvement, and the entire teaching of the Scriptures is in harmony with the declaration of the wise man, that *it is not good for the soul to be without knowledge.* Prov. xix, 2. *For wisdom*, he says, *is better than rubies, and all the things that may be desired are not to be compared to it.* Prov. viii, 11.

On the false assumption that the acquisition of knowledge has a tendency to weaken the religious sensibilities; or, as the proverb has it, that ignorance is the mother of devotion, the Romish Church discourages the study of the Bible, and impiously seeks to nullify the command of Christ to *search the Scriptures.* John v, 39.

But this is not all. The human mind is immortal. When it passes from the body it enters upon a realm where, beginning at the point reached in this world, it may still pursue its studies and increase its stores of knowledge.

A little girl made her appearance for the first time last Sunday in the infant class.

She is very ignorant, six years old, and don't know a single letter. She is an orphan. Her father she never knew, and her mother died only a week ago. The superintendent talked with her. She was not at all bashful, but rather rude. She did not know who made her, and had never heard of the Bible or of heaven. The poor child was bare-footed and her dress was ragged. Our treasurer fitted her with a new pair of shoes, and the female superintendent gave her a frock and bonnet. She did not seem to know enough to say thank you for these things.

This exceedingly ignorant child has a mind capable of receiving knowledge. Her duty, if she can be made to understand her duty, is to cultivate her intellect, and no one can tell how brightly that intellect, now so dim and dull, may shine.

There must be a limit to the attainments she can possibly make, for hers is but a finite intellect; yet who may say unto her, Thus far mayst thou go, but no further? Enlightened by careful and patient instruction, taken by the hand of Christian affection and led to the cross of Christ, taught everything that her faculties can grasp in this world, we may follow that intellect, now so dull and dark, into the realm where the great Teacher himself leads his disciples to *living fountains of waters*, (Rev. vii, 17,) and there, from the lips of this forsaken friendless orphan may yet be heard the triumphant outburst of the poet:

> Now then I see, and hear, and know
> All I desired or wished below;
> While every power finds sweet employ
> In this eternal world of joy.

Questions on Lesson XX.

1. What is the subject now to be considered?
2. What is said not to be possible?
3. How near may we approach a state of physical perfection?
4. What is the result as we approach it?
5. To what is it not possible to set limits?
6. Wherein is most of the Creator's glory revealed?
7. What is it said that we cannot conceive?
8. Is it possible for man to go beyond the attainments yet made?
9. What is it said we may easily conceive?
10. What duty is thence inferred?
11. What is said of the notion that knowledge and religion are incompatible?
12. What is the quotation from Proverbs?

13. What is said to be in harmony with it?
14. Can you repeat Proverbs viii, 11?
15. What does the Church of Rome discourage?
16. Why?
17. What command of Christ is thereby nullified?
18. What is said of the mind after the death of the body?
19. Can you relate what is said of the orphan girl?
20. Of what is the mind of this ignorant girl capable?
21. What is her duty?
22. Why must there be a limit to her attainments?
23. Who can fix that limit?
24. What may be her future?
25. Repeat Revelation vii, 17.

LESSON TWENTY-FIRST.

CULTIVATION OF THE INTELLECT—CONTINUED.

When the great Wesley said, "I reverence a little child," he had in his mind the capabilities of the intellect given to it by the Creator. Like the orphan girl mentioned in the last lesson, every child who comes into this world in the enjoyment of the intellectual faculties is capable of improving them to an indefinite extent. The duty of so doing is proved, first, by the fact that we have this capability. If it were not intended to be improved it would not have been imparted, for nothing is clearer than that the infinitely wise God does nothing in vain or without a purpose. The brute creation have not this capability, and therefore such improvement is not expected from them.

In the second place, no matter what may be our present attainments, there is room for progressive advancement. You know a great deal more than that ignorant child who never heard of God or of heaven until last Sunday; and yet there are a great many things you do not know, and of which you are as ignorant as she is. It is as much your duty as it is hers to seek knowledge and to cultivate the intellect.

Thirdly, our usefulness to our fellow-creatures, as well as our individual happiness, greatly depends upon the improvement of the mind.

In all the history of our race we find that those who have been most highly esteemed as the benefactors of mankind have been the studious and the intellectually diligent. It is an admitted fact, too, that, next to the love of God shed abroad in the heart, there is no greater happiness to be attained than the expansion of the intellect by the acquisition of knowledge.

And once again, it is a well-established fact, that if the mind does not enlarge and expand by the acquisition of knowledge it will inevitably dwindle and become feeble. Like the limbs of the body, the powers of the mind strengthen by exercise and become weak by disuse.

As to the means of mental improvement, Solomon said, nearly three thousand years ago, *He that walketh with wise men shall be wise*, (Prov. xiii, 20;) and an old proverb of our own says, Tell me with whom you go and I'll tell you what you do. It is a law of the human mind to imitate and become like those with whom we keep company. When it is in our power we should choose the society of the studious and the thoughtful, of those who will help rather than of those who will hinder us in the attainment of knowledge and the cultivation of intellect.

Then, again, the world is full of the results of thought and study. It was long since said, *Of making many books there is no end.* Ecc. xii, 12. And yet they continue to be made for the purpose of feeding the mind and conveying instruction. To say nothing of books designed for this object, in schools and academies there are volumes within everybody's reach on almost every subject. If you do not *give attendance to reading*, as Paul directed Timothy to do, (1 Tim. iv, 13,) it will not be for want of books; nor, unless yours is a very peculiar case, for want of opportunity. The fault will most certainly be your own, and yours too will be the regret if you allow the best part of your life to pass away without mental improvement. It is a sad thing to discover in mature years, amid the pressing cares of active life, that, owing to neglect in youth, the mind has lost its relish for knowledge and has now no inclination for study.

By reading something more is to be understood than the mere perusal of books. A great many pages may be hurried over without profit. Thus to read is like cramming the stomach with food which if it be not digested is an injury rather than a benefit. The food of the mind needs to be digested as well as that of the body.

The parallel between the body and the mind may be continued still further. All food is not wholesome; some books are pernicious. In the one case as in the other, poison may be concealed under a fair exterior. It is a duty we owe to ourselves to be even more cautious with reference to improper mental aliment than to unwholesome natural food, because the evil effects of the former are less readily perceived than those of the latter, while they are more pernicious and less easily counteracted.

Questions on Lesson XXI.

1. What saying of the great Wesley's is here quoted?
2. What induced that saying?
3. What is said of every child that comes into the world?
4. What does the possession of this faculty prove?
5. What if it were not intended to be improved?
6. What is said of the brute creation?
7. What is the second argument?
8. What comparison is made between you and that little child?
9. Upon what does our usefulness and happiness greatly depend?
10. What classes of men have been the greatest benefactors of their race?
11. What is said of happiness?
12. What is the fourth argument?
13. Wherein do the powers of the mind resemble the limbs of the body?

14. What saying of Solomon's is quoted as to the means of mental improvement?
15. What says the old proverb on the subject?
16. On what law of the human mind are these proverbs founded?
17. Whose society should we prefer?
18. For what purpose are books prepared and published?
19. How do you understand the quotation from Ecc. xii, 12?
20. What is Paul's direction to Timothy?
21. If that advice is not heeded, whose will be the fault?
22. What is said to be a sad thing?
23. What is to be understood by reading?
24. To what is the rapid perusal of books compared?
25. What needs to be digested?
26. Wherein is the parallel further seen?
27. Why should we be more careful of mental than of bodily food?

LESSON TWENTY-SECOND.

THE MORAL FACULTIES.

By many teachers of moral science, and in most of the text-books on the subject, one great fact is overlooked or kept out of sight. That fact is the natural depravity of the human heart. Our own reflection and observation, as well as the teachings of the Bible, assure us that by nature man is very different from what he was when he came from the hands of his Maker. Adam's natural instinct was to do right; every impulse was toward the good and the true. But how is it with us? We find within our hearts a propensity to do wrong, a disposition that prefers evil to good, and a constant bias to practices which even our own consciences condemn.

We see the same in our fellow-creatures, even in little children, as well as among our class-mates and play-mates. In reading accounts of voyages and travels, we find that this is also the case with people in other parts of the world, in civilized countries and in savage lands.

The book of God confirms the truth of our own observation. *The imagination of man's heart is evil from his youth.* Gen. viii, 21. *They go astray as soon as they be born, speaking lies.* Psalm lviii, 3. *There is none that doeth good. They are all gone aside, they are all together become filthy: there is none that doeth good, no, not one.* Psalm xiv, 1, 3.

Numerous other texts might be cited from the Old Testament, and the New Testament is full of the same doctrine. We quote but one passage. It is that in which the Apostle Paul uses the sentiment of the psalmist, clothing it in his own more nervous and expressive language: *There is none righteous, no, not one: there is none that understandeth, there is none that seeketh after God. They are all gone out of the way, they are together become unprofitable; there is none that doeth good, no, not one.* Rom. iii, 11, 12.

These teachings, it will be perceived, admit of no exceptional cases. Our own experience, so far as it goes, attests the fact. There is no exception. The children of the rich differ not from the children of the poor. Those who have the benefits of education are, in this respect, precisely on a level with those who grope in ignorance.

The cultivation of the intellect may be carried to an indefinite extent without producing any beneficial effect upon the heart. On the contrary, it is a possible case that man's moral nature may be depraved just in proportion, and just to that degree in which his intellectual powers have been cultivated and his mind enlightened.

Hence, there can be no question so full of interest, and none of so much importance to a rational creature, as that which refers to the possibility of purifying the moral nature. May this propensity to evil be eradicated? Are there any means by which I may regain what Adam had and lost—a love for the true, the right, and the good? Certainly there can be no duty which I owe to myself so important, so imperative as the duty of satisfactorily solving these questions. And they are of easy solution. Light has been poured upon them, light from the central glory of the universe, the cross of Christ.

Having rejoiced in this light, as is your privilege and your duty, the path of moral improvement opens plainly before you. *It is a path that shineth more and more unto the perfect day.* Prov. iv, 18. Then, in the language of the psalmist, you may *go from strength to strength*, (Psalm lxxxiv, 7,) and by making use of the means put within your reach, you may *grow in grace and in the knowledge of our Lord and Saviour Jesus Christ.* 2 Peter iii, 18.

Other means of grace will be noticed hereafter. At present we mention two only as incumbent upon those who ask, What is my duty to myself with reference to the strengthening of my moral faculties? They are the reading of God's word, and the hearing it expounded from the pulpit.

Not a day should pass without reading some portion of the Bible. Not an opportunity of hearing it preached should be willingly neglected.

Questions on Lesson XXII.

1. What is said of many teachers of moral science?
2. What fact is kept out of sight?
3. What does observation assure us?
4. What teaches the same truth?
5. What was the natural instinct of Adam?
6. What do we find in our hearts?
7. Where else do we see this?
8. Is it found to be the same in children?
9. How is it in other parts of the world?
10. Can you quote some passages from the Bible on this subject?
11. What is Paul's language in Rom. iii, 11, 12?
12. Are there not some exceptions?
13. What effect does the cultivation of the intellect produce on the heart?
14. What is said to be a possible case?
15. What is said of the possibility of purifying the moral nature?

16. What is the most important duty I owe to myself?
17. Can those questions be answered?
18. Whence comes the answer?
19. What follows the reception of this light?
20. What passage is quoted from Proverbs?
21. What from the Psalms?
22. What from Saint Peter?
23. What means of grace are specially noticed?
24. What is said of the Bible and of preaching?

LESSON TWENTY-THIRD.

THE GOLDEN RULE.

OUR duties to one another are summed up in the rule of conduct laid down by Jesus Christ: *All things whatsoever ye would that men should do to you, do ye even so to them.* Matt. vii, 12.

This is called the golden rule. It is so called because of its value and utility, and these are seen in the fact that it comprises a whole system of morality in a few words easily understood and readily remembered.

It is a rule of universal application. At all times, in youth, in manhood, and in old age; under all circumstances, by the monarch and the beggar, in the city and in the country, on sea and on land, it is alike and equally applicable.

The justice and propriety of the golden rule appeal to the common sense of mankind. Let it be understood, and the savage of the wilderness admits its propriety as readily as the man of refined and cultivated intellect. The heathen sees its beauty and simplicity, and the avowed skeptic and the infidel admit its beneficial tendency.

Before entering upon the specific obligations growing out of this rule and founded upon it, let us dwell a little upon the rule itself. And first, you perceive that it is broad and unqualified. In all things do unto others as you would have them do unto you. In any supposable circumstances, if you would ascertain your duty to your fellow, in imagination change places with him, and your own duty is at once made plain.

But while there is no exception in this view of the subject, the golden rule sets limits to our wishes and expectations from others. We have no right to ask from any one what, under a change of circumstances, we should be unwilling or unable to give.

THE BOARDING-SCHOOL GIRLS.

A man, for instance, has been tried for a criminal offense. He has been found guilty; and now, just as the judge is about to pronounce the sentence that will send him to prison, the culprit reminds him of the golden rule. "If you were in my place," says he, "you would like to be set free." But the judge has duties and responsibilities to society which no one has a right to ask him to violate. He cannot decline to pass sentence upon the criminal without neglecting a duty which he has promised, perhaps sworn, faithfully to perform.

Somewhat similar was the case between two girls at a large boarding school. They were bosom friends. They kept no secrets from each other, and had promised mutual assistance in all cases of trouble or difficulty. One of the girls, it is not necessary to mention her name, had been tempted to the commission of a serious offense against the known rules of the seminary. No one knew of it but her bosom friend, and it so happened that the teacher questioned her on the subject. What ought she to do? If she tells the truth the guilty one will be disgraced and punished. If she tells a falsehood, possibly, although that is not certain, the disgrace and punishment will be averted. Of course the answer is very easy. To tell the truth is a paramount duty. No one has a right to utter a falsehood to save himself from punishment nor to expect another to do it for him.

And so with all other positive duties which we owe to ourselves, to one another, and to our Maker. We have no right to violate one of them under the plea of doing as we would be done by, for we have no right to desire others to do anything of the kind for us.

We may see now how the golden rule is calculated to put an end to all covetousness and inordinate self-esteem. Can any one desire another to violate conscience for his sake so long as he has a determination to do to others as he would have others do to him?

If I covet the possessions of another and would still obey the golden rule, must I not give to him just as much as I require, and thus precisely balance the account between us? A child can see the bearing of the golden rule in this respect, and put to shame the cavils of those who try to throw ridicule upon it.

"You want me," said little Edward to his brother, "you want me to give you my humming top. Well, you must do as you would be done by, and give me yours."

Questions on Lesson XXIII.

1. What is the rule of conduct laid down by Christ in Matt. vii, 12?
2. What is it called?
3. Why is it so called?
4. What does it comprise?
5. When and where is it applicable?
6. What is said of its justice and propriety?
7. What is said of the savage of the wilderness?
8. What is said of the heathen?
9. What of the skeptic and the infidel?
10. What is the first remark concerning this rule?
11. How are you to ascertain your duty to your fellow?
12. To what does this rule set limits?
13. What have we no right to ask from others?
14. Give the illustration?
15. Why may not the judge decline to sentence the criminal?
16. What is said of the agreement entered into by two girls at boarding school?
17. Can you relate the circumstances and the conclusion?
18. What have we no right to do?

19. What is the golden rule calculated to put an end to?
20. How is this exhibited?
21. 'What was little Edward's illustration?

LESSON TWENTY-FOURTH.

VIOLATIONS OF THE GOLDEN RULE.

In general terms it may be said that the golden rule is violated by every species of injustice. Nobody desires to be unjustly dealt with, and consequently he who treats another with injustice does as he would not be done by.

1. Nations are guilty in this respect when the strong wage war against the weak, and in any way oppress them. God takes cognizance of national sins, and will surely punish for them. Necessarily, inasmuch as nations cannot be summoned before his bar and punished in their collective capacity in another world, their punishment must fall upon them in the present. And God has many methods of taking vengeance. War, pestilence, and famine are his

ministers. At his nod the mightiest nation may be dashed in pieces like a potter's vessel. Our only hope for the perpetuity of our country's glory must rest upon obedience to the requirements of Jehovah, and punishment for national sins can only be averted by penitence on the part of individuals. It is a blessed truth that it may be thus averted, otherwise sudden destruction might fall upon a people for some gross act of wickedness on the part of their rulers and legislators. See God's gracious assurance in this respect. Jeremiah xviii, 7, 8.

2. THE SLAVE-TRADE is a violation of the golden rule on the part of all who engage in it and of all who connive at it. This is too plain to need an argument, and the laws of the United States regard the trade, when carried on in foreign lands, as equivalent to piracy, a crime punishable with death among all civilized people. Of course the traffic in our own country is equally wrong. In many aspects it is worse. It is attended frequently with circumstances of greater hardship in the forcible sundering of family ties and the disruption of social and religious enjoyments. Any argument against stealing a heathen from the coast of Africa

must have at least equal force against selling, for gain, a native born American, whatever may be the color of his skin.

3. THE BUYING, SELLING, OR HOLDING OF HUMAN BEINGS TO BE USED AS CHATTELS is inconsistent with the golden rule. So says the Discipline of the Church, and so say the Scriptures and common sense. No human being not imbruted below the level of a dumb beast *can* desire to be the slave of another. If he could he would have no right to choose that relationship, inasmuch as thereby he would rob his unborn offspring of what the Declaration of American Independence pronounces an inalienable right, namely, liberty. Most assuredly he who exercises the right of ownership over a human being as he would over a horse or a piece of land, does as he would not be done by.

4. TO TAKE ADVANTAGE OF ANOTHER'S POVERTY, TO OPPRESS THE HIRELING, OR TO DENY HIM FAIR AND EQUITABLE WAGES is a species of the same kind of injustice; and he who does it knows that he is not doing to others as he would have others do unto him. There is a vast amount of this kind of injustice and wrong-doing even among

professedly moral people; and some who are most vehement in their denunciations of the great evil of slavery are not guiltless in this respect.

The provisions of the Levitical law were very pointed on this subject, and the teachings of the New Testament are of the same import. *Thou shalt not oppress a hired servant that is poor and needy, whether he be of thy brethren, or of thy strangers that are in thy land within thy gates. At his day thou shalt give him his hire, neither shall the sun go down upon it, for he is poor, and setteth his heart upon it: lest he cry against thee unto the Lord, and it be sin unto thee.* Deut. xxiv, 14, 15. *Go to now, ye rich men, weep and howl for your miseries that shall come upon you. Behold, the hire of the laborers who have reaped down your fields, which is of you kept back by fraud, crieth; and the cries of them which have reaped are entered into the ears of the Lord of Sabbaoth.* James v, 1, 4.

5. The same is true of all who TAKE ADVANTAGE OF THE IGNORANCE OF OTHERS, AND CHEAT THEM IN BUYING OR SELLING. Nobody likes to be cheated. Every one who swerves

in ever so slight a degree from the straight path of justice in his dealings does to that extent violate the golden rule.

Questions on Lesson XXIV.

1. In general terms how is the golden rule said to be violated?
2. What follows from the fact that nobody desires to be unjustly dealt with?
3. What is the first illustration?
4. What is said of national sins?
5. When are national sins punished?
6. Why?
7. What are some of God's methods of punishing nations?
8. On what rests the hope of our country's continued prosperity?
9. How is vengeance for national sins to be averted?
10. Can you repeat Jeremiah xviii, 7, 8?
11. What is said of the slave-trade?
12. How do the laws regard the foreign slave-trade?
13. What of the traffic in our own country?
14. What is the third specification?
15. Can a human being desire to be a slave?
16. Why has he not a right to desire that relationship?
17. What is the next violation of the golden rule here mentioned?

GIRL IN DISTRESS.

18. What says the law of Moses on this subject?
19. What says St. James?
20. What is said of those who cheat in buying and selling?

LESSON TWENTY-FIFTH.

VIOLATIONS OF THE GOLDEN RULE—CONTINUED.

THERE are many methods by which the golden rule is violated, in addition to those which are so clearly seen to come under the head of palpable injustice. Among them may be mentioned:

1. *Refusing assistance to a fellow-creature when it is in our power to grant it.* Here the claim is not for justice, but for mercy.

When the child of want, hungry and cold, stands shivering before me; or the panting fugitive from the house of bondage knocks at the door and begs for shelter and for bread, then Christ's golden rule tells me, in imagination to change places with him and to do as I would be done by. No human enactment can abrogate this duty, and no plea of expediency can release from its performance.

2. Treating the poor with contempt because of their poverty is a very frequent offense, and one most pointedly rebuked in the sacred Scriptures. *The rich and poor*, it is said, *meet together: the Lord is the maker of them all*, (Prov. xxii, 2,) that is, both conditions are equally in the order of God's providence, and both classes are of equal importance in his sight. Hence it is said again, *Whoso mocketh*, that is, ridiculeth, or treateth with contempt, *the poor*, *reproacheth his Maker*. Prov. xvii, 5. The apostle James is indignantly severe upon the professing Christians of his day, whom he charges with having *despised the poor*. James ii. 6. It will be a profitable employment, and may be of service to you in future life, to commit to memory the preceding verses, that is, verses one to five of the second chapter of James.

3. *Judging harshly of conduct and imputing it to the worst motives.* A felon at the bar of justice, when on trial for a crime that may send him to the penitentiary or even to the gallows, is always supposed to be innocent until he is proved guilty. Dur-

ing all the trial he has the benefit of every doubt. Christ says, *with what judgment ye judge ye shall be judged, and with what measure ye mete it shall be measured to you again.* Matt. vii, 2. And it would be well if we might always make the prayer of the poet our own and be satisfied to have it literally answered:

"The mercy I to others show
That mercy show to me."

4. *Unnecessarily exposing another's faults and failings* is a very common mode of violating this rule. We have seen that we may not tell a falsehood to screen the guilty. It is little better to tell the truth to the injury of another without a sufficient reason for so doing. What that sufficient reason may be every one must determine for himself. If the cause of justice demands an exposure of another's faults, no fear of being called a tell-tale ought to prevent it. But if it is done merely in sport, or to gratify a love of mischief, or a feeling of hatred or envy, of course it is wrong.

5. *Ridiculing the peculiarities of another's person or appearance.* It is a very easy thing to give a boy or a girl a disagree-

able nick-name, and to render a child very unhappy by making his dress, or the color of his hair, or the peculiar conformation of any of his features a subject of ridicule. There may be more wickedness in other violations of the golden rule, but none so mean and inexcusable. The boy or the girl who indulges in this propensity reminds one of the madman spoken of by Solomon who *scattereth firebrands, arrows, and death, and saith, Am I not in sport?* Prov. xxvi, 18, 19.

Questions on Lesson XXV.

1. What is the subject of this lesson?
2. What is the introductory statement?
3. What violation is first mentioned?
4. What illustrations are given?
5. What is the next offense mentioned?
6. Explain Proverbs xxii, 2.
7. What is said of him that mocketh the poor?
8. What do you understand by mocking the poor?
9. What does St. James charge those to whom he wrote with doing?
10. Can you repeat James ii, 1–5?
11. What is the third violation of the golden rule here mentioned?
12. What is said of a prisoner at the bar of justice?

13. Repeat Christ's declaration as found in Matthew vii, 2.
14. What is the prayer of the poet?
15. What violation of the golden rule is next mentioned?
16. Is this a common mode of violating the golden rule?
17. What may we not do to screen the guilty?
18. What is said to be but little better than telling a falsehood to screen the guilty?
19. Who is to decide what is a sufficient reason?
20. When the cause of justice demands it, what is to be done?
21. What other violation of the golden rule is mentioned?
22. What is said to be a very easy thing?
23. What is the character of this violation of the golden rule?

LESSON TWENTY-SIXTH.

SECOND QUARTERLY REVISION.

WITH this lesson we finish the first half of the volume. The student, it is hoped, will be able readily to answer the questions here proposed and any others that may be asked by the teacher. We confine ourselves to the lessons from the fourteenth to the twenty-fifth inclusive; but scholars ought to be able to answer any questions founded on the lessons from the beginning of the volume.

1. What is the foundation of moral obligation?
2. How is the will of God revealed to us?
3. Distinguish between self-love and selfishness.
4. Repeat, in your own language, the story of Felix.
5. How do you prove that the body may be sinned against?
6. Relate what is said of the girl who chewed India rubber.
7. Do you know what India rubber is?
8. What is said of idleness in the first sentence of lesson sixteenth?
9. What are essential conditions of health?
10. What employment did God give to Adam before his fall?
11. What evinces the Creator's original design in man's creation?
12. Repeat the fourth commandment.
13. What is said of the apostle Paul's industrious habits?
14. How is the fact illustrated that industry is not confined to bodily labor?
15. What class of diversions is first men-

tioned as precluded by the General Rules of the Church?

16. Why are dancing and theatrical entertainments prohibited?
17. Why should we shun some amusements that are not in themselves sinful?
18. What three subjects are connected in the eighteenth lesson?
19. What besides immoderate drinking is included in temperance?
20. What is said of the immoderate pursuit of things in themselves desirable?
21. What frequently results from the immoderate pursuit of knowledge?
22. Relate the anecdote of the rich man and his farm.
23. State the reasons that should induce us to be contented with our lot in life.
24. What may every one find in the dispensations of Providence?
25. How is our capacity of enjoyment increased?
26. To what is it impossible to set limits?
27. What is revealed in the study of the human mind?
28. What is said of Newton?
29. For what purpose were our mental capabilities imparted by the Creator?

30. Repeat what you remember about the orphan girl mentioned in lesson twentieth.
31. State the arguments by which is proved the duty of cultivating the intellectual powers.
32. To what may reading without proper reflection be compared?
33. What is essential to make reading profitable?
34. Mention some particulars in which food for the mind resembles food for the body.
35. What do you understand by natural depravity?
36. How is the existence of natural depravity proved?
37. Does cultivation of the intellect always tend to improve the heart?
38. What is the golden rule?
39. By whom was it laid down?
40. What is said of the applicability of the golden rule?
41. What good effects would result from the general observance of this rule?
42. Of what are nations guilty when they wage war against those weaker than themselves?

43. In what respects is the domestic slave-trade as bad as the foreign?
44. What says the Discipline of the Church on the subject of slaveholding?
45. Of what kind of injustice is there said to be a vast amount?
46. Lesson twenty-fourth mentions five varieties of injustice by which the golden rule is violated: what are they?
47. What are the violations of this rule mentioned in the twenty-fifth lesson?
48. Can you prove that industry is a duty?

LESSON TWENTY-SEVENTH.

EXPEDIENCY.

UNDER the plea of expediency, violations of the golden rule, and other acts of disobedience, as well as omissions of known duty, are sometimes excused and justified. By example, as well as precept, the teachings of the Bible are sufficiently clear on this subject.

The three Hebrew children, of whom we have an account in the book of Daniel, were commanded by an idolatrous tyrant to bow down and worship a golden image. The penalty of disobedience was death, a most horrid death, that of being cast into a furnace of fire. Many even in this day would have said, When life may be saved so easily, by such a simple act as bending the knee to an idol, it is expedient to do so, and thus escape the terrible consequences. But God had positively forbidden the act required by the king, and these men preferred to obey him, and God took care of them.

Suppose that in his wisdom the Almighty had not interfered for their deliverance, and that they had been burned alive. Even in that case we cannot but see that their conduct would have been wise as well as right, and that in fact the result of that conduct has nothing to do with the question of the expediency of doing what God has forbidden.

Take another illustration. A farmer has a large field of grain just ready for the sickle. On the Lord's day threatening clouds portend a heavy shower. Self-interest says, Summon your men and secure the grain before it is all spoiled. But God says, *Thou shalt not do any work on the Sabbath*, and it is the farmer's duty to obey God, and no plea of expediency can excuse the guilt of doing what he has forbidden.

Mary had a long lesson in geography to recite on Monday morning. The result of that recitation was to decide which of three candidates should have the gold medal. It so happened that all Saturday was occupied by household duties; and at night company came in, which prevented her from even looking at the lesson. On Sunday morning she went to church, and as there was no service in the afternoon, Mary's first thought was to devote that time to her geography; but she remembered what God had said about the Sabbath day. So she sat down and read her Bible, and tried to keep the day holy. The result was, that when one of her competitors was rewarded with the medal Mary had a feeling of far greater satisfaction than she could have had if by violating the Lord's day she had succeeded in obtaining it.

In a former lesson we considered the case of a physician who was at the bedside of a very sick man. The doctor thought the man would soon die, and in that opinion he was correct. But when the patient sought to know the truth he withheld it, from what he deemed motives of expediency, and deliberately uttered a falsehood. The man died, and the doctor was sorry that he did not tell him the truth. But if the result had been different, and a rapid recovery had followed the falsehood, it is clear that the physician would not have been thereby justified, and that, in fact, his guilt would have been precisely the same.

The general principle is, that expediency can never be a valid excuse for doing what is in itself wrong. Of two courses of conduct, either of which is equally proper, expediency may settle the question of choice between them; or of two or more methods of performing the same duty, we are at liberty to take that which at the time seems most desirable.

In the case of the physician, expediency might have settled the question as to the manner of telling the disagreeable truth to the dying man; and so as respects Mary and her lesson in geography, expediency, while it could not have justified doing what God has forbidden, might have determined her choice between two or three different courses. As, for instance, she was at liberty to do as she did; or to have excused herself to the company on Saturday night, and to have devoted the time to study; or to have risen very early on Monday morning for that purpose.

Questions on Lesson XXVII.

1. Under what plea are violations of duty sometimes excused?
2. What is said of the teachings of the Bible on this subject?
3. Which commandment were the Hebrew children commanded to violate?
4. By whom?
5. What was the penalty of disobedience?
6. Suppose they had been burned alive: what then?
7. Relate the case of the farmer?
8. What cannot a plea of expediency excuse?
9. What was Mary's geography lesson to decide?
10. What hindered her from study on Saturday night?
11. Why did she not study it on Sunday?
12. How did she employ her time on Sunday?
13. How did she feel when another obtained the prize?
14. What is said of the doctor and the sick man?
15. What is the general principle?
16. What question may expediency settle?
17. What are we at liberty to do when there are two or more methods of performing the same duty?
18. How is this illustrated in the case of the physician?
19. How in the case of Mary?
20. What three courses would have been proper?

LESSON TWENTY-EIGHTH.

EXPEDIENCY—CONTINUED.

We have seen that expediency can never justify the doing of anything that God has forbidden. It is also true that no plea of expediency is sufficient to excuse from the performance of a duty that is enjoined upon us. An illustration of this principle is found in the conduct of the prophet Daniel, (ch. vi,) who, when forbidden to pray under the threatened punishment of death, *went into his house, and his windows being open in his chamber toward Jerusalem, he knelt upon his knees three times a day, and prayed, and gave thanks before his God, as he did aforetime.* Verse 10. Imagination can scarcely picture a case where a spurious expediency could have suggested more reasons for the omission of duty. Surely, it might have urged, it is a vastly important matter to save life, and it is an exceedingly little thing to suspend prayer for a season. And then, why not pray in secret? Why perform the duty three times a day with the same regularity as before the decree was issued? At any rate, why not shut the windows? Or, in short, why not refrain from prayer and obey the law? for be it remembered that the will of the despot was the law of the land. Not one of these questions seems to have occurred to Daniel, and the Holy Spirit has left his course of conduct on record among *the things which were written aforetime for our learning.* Rom. xv, 4.

But this is not the teaching of the Old Testament merely. The conduct of the two apostles, Peter and John, as recorded in the fourth chapter of the Acts, is very similar to that of Daniel, and conveys even a keener rebuke to those professing Christians who evade the performance of a known duty on the plea of expediency.

Filled with the Holy Ghost these men had been performing miracles and preaching to the people the doctrine of Christ's resurrection from the dead. For this the authorities had apprehended and imprisoned them. They bore their imprisonment with patience, without railing against those who thus treated them, or even questioning their authority. Having punished them, as the rulers thought, sufficiently, they were about to set them at liberty, but before doing so they *commanded them not to speak at all, nor teach in the name of Jesus.* Verse 18. These rulers had the power to punish for disobedience still more severely, but the apostles told them that they intended to do as they had been doing, challenging them to deny the truth of the proposition that God is to be obeyed rather than man, (verse 19 and ch., v. 29,) and thus teaching that when the laws of the land come in conflict with the law of God the latter is to be obeyed at all hazards.

As in the case of refraining from what God has forbidden, so, in that of doing what he has commanded, expediency has nothing to do with the settlement of the question whether it shall be done or be left undone. It can never be a valid excuse for doing what is wrong, nor a justification for the omission of a known duty.

Expediency might have settled the duty of Peter and John as to what answer should be given to the magistrates, or whether any answer at all should be given; and so with doing anything not forbidden, or leaving undone anything not enjoined. For expediency's sake Paul would eat no meat if thereby his brother should be made to stumble; and although the mere taste of alcohol is not in itself sinful, yet, inasmuch as nobody is commanded to drink it, it may be the dictate of a wise expediency totally to abstain, lest, induced by our example, others are led into intemperance.

It follows from what has been said that two duties can never clash; that is, that it cannot be binding upon us at the same time to obey two contradictory commands. In the cases last referred to, that of Daniel and that of the apostles, for instance, there might seem at first to be a question as to the proper path of duty. Submission to rulers might have been urged in both cases as a religious duty, as it certainly is; but obedience to God is a higher duty, to which the lesser must always yield.

Finally, let it be observed that in these and all similar cases there must be positive certainty as to what is duty. If the apostles had been in doubt as to the propriety of their course in preaching to the people they would not have been justified in their bold language to the magistrates, and it would have been no better than a foolhardy risk of his life if Daniel had braved the wrath of the tyrant for anything less than positive certainty as to the will of God. Those who seek to know that they may do his will have little difficulty in ascertaining it.

Questions on Lesson XXVIII.

1. What did the preceding lesson teach us?
2. What is here said to be also true?
3. From whom is the first illustration taken?
4. What did Daniel do as related in ch. vi, 10?
5. What is said of a spurious expediency in this case?
6. What might it have urged?
7. In what way might his prayers have been offered?
8. What other questions might have been suggested?
9. What was the law of the land?
10. Why was Daniel's conduct left on record?
11. Is there a similar illustration in the New Testament?
12. Where is it recorded?
13. Relate it.
14. What does their conduct convey?
15. What is to be done when the laws of man come in conflict with the law of God?
16. With what has expediency nothing to do?
17. What question might expediency have settled?
18. What, for expediency's sake, would Paul not do?
19. Is there any command to drink intoxicating liquors?

20. What then is the dictate of expediency in that matter?
21. What inference is drawn from the subject?
22. What is said to be a religious duty?
23. What is said of obedience to God?
24. In these and similar cases what must there always be?
25. How is this illustrated?
26. What is said of those who seek to know his will?

LESSON TWENTY-NINTH.

THE COMMANDMENT WITH PROMISE.

In the Bible the special duties of children to parents are inculcated with great frequency and solemnity. Among the commandments issued by the Almighty from Mount Sinai, that which directs you to honor your father and your mother has the first place in what is called the second table. The four preceding commandments have reference to God and his worship. They are immediately followed by what the apostle calls the commandment with promise. It is in these words: *Honor thy father and thy mother, that thy days may be long upon the land which the Lord thy God giveth thee.*

This commandment is of course equally binding upon all who have parents; and in the case of orphan children, from whom death has taken both father and mother, those who perform the parents' part as guardians or protectors are entitled to the honor due to parents.

Father and mother are both included in the command, and are both entitled to equal honor. A very foolish question is sometimes asked of little children: Which do you love best? It was answered, not grammatically, but pointedly and forcibly, by a boy five years of age. "I love them both," said he; "both as much as one, and one as much as both."

The duty is not made to depend upon the character or disposition of parents. They may be unkind, morose, or even immoral. The duty is to honor them because they are parents, not because of the kindness of their disposition, nor on account of any moral quality they may possess.

No limit is set as to the time when this duty ceases to be binding. It is not a command to little children merely, but to them and to all others whose fathers or mothers are living. The duty becomes more imperative as children grow older; the parents begin to feel the infirmities of age, and there is something exceedingly pleasing in witnessing honor paid to parents by sons and daughters after they themselves have grown up to be men and women.

The honor thus required to be shown to parents includes love, gratitude, reverence, and obedience.

To love one's father and mother seems to be nothing more than a natural instinct, and so with gratitude. Henry's dog evidently loves him, as he shows in the best way he can by jumping and frisking about him when he comes home from school. He seems to evince something like gratitude, too, by his conduct toward those who have done him a favor. If such be the fact with dumb brutes, and the prophet says that even *the ox knoweth his owner, and the ass his master's crib*, (Isaiah i, 3,) it would be strange indeed if a child did not love those to whom, under God, he owes his being and everything he has; and gratitude is but one of the many means by which love is made manifest. In this case it is a disposition to make such returns as are possible for the innumerable favors that have been received.

There is a man of my acquaintance who has for many years labored for the support of his aged father, who was defrauded of his property, and rendered incapable of any work by a sad accident. This man does no more than his duty; and yet, in addition to the pleasing consciousness of well-doing, which is an ample reward for his toil, his name is never mentioned but with respect by those who know him.

By the reverence due to parents is to be understood that submissive deference which always looks upon a father and a mother as superiors. A child may have a great deal more education, be more graceful in manners, and in process of time become more honored in the community; but still, if correctly instructed, will regard himself as inferior by virtue of that relationship which God himself has established, and will always reverence his father and his mother. It is written in the book of Leviticus, (xix, 3,) *Ye shall fear every man his mother and his father;* and the apostle Paul, speaking of our fathers, says, *We gave them reverence.* Heb. xii, 9.

In the history of Joseph, as written in the book of Genesis, there is a beautiful illustration of filial love, and gratitude, and reverence. The acknowledged ruler of Egypt supplies all the wants of his father when famine stares him in the face, falls into his arms and sheds tears of joy when they meet after being so long separated, and when the poor old man is on his death-bed, the governor seeks reverently his blessing for himself and his children.

Questions on Lesson XXIX.

1. What are inculcated with great frequency in the Bible?
2. Which command has the first place in the second table?
3. To what do the first four commandments refer?
4. What is the fifth commandment called?
5. Repeat it.
6. Upon whom is this command binding?
7. What is said of orphans?
8. Is any difference made between father and mother?
9. What foolish question is sometimes asked of children?
10. On what is it said the duty does not depend?
11. Why are they to be honored?
12. Is the command addressed to little children merely?

13. What of the duty as children grow older?
14. What is said to be exceedingly pleasing?
15. What is included in the honor required to be shown to parents?
16. What is said of a natural instinct?
17. What is said of Henry's dog?
18. What says the prophet about dumb animals?
19. How is gratitude here defined?
20. State what is said of a grateful son.
21. What do you mean by the reverence due to parents?
22. What is written in Leviticus xix, 3?
23. What is said of Joseph?

LESSON THIRTIETH.

FILIAL OBEDIENCE.

THE duty of *obedience* to parents is included in the *honor* required to be paid to them by the fifth commandment. It is the foundation of the whole. Professions of love are a mockery, and pretended reverence is a sham, if not accompanied by obedience. *Children, obey your parents in the Lord, for this is right.* Ephes. vi, 1. *Children, obey your parents in all things, for this is well pleasing unto the Lord.* Col.

iii, 20. Such are the specific injunctions of the word of God. They are addressed to children because, unlike the other duties of love, and gratitude, and reverence, which are always binding, implicit obedience ceases to be required when a child arrives at maturity and begins to act upon his own responsibility. Until that time, however, the duty is to obey in all things. Of course this does not include things forbidden by God. A parent has no right to command any violation of His law; and if such a command should be given, the child is under obligations to disobey it and take the consequences. Hence the command, Obey your parents *in all things*, is modified and explained in the parallel passage, Obey your parents *in the Lord*, that is, in everything not forbidden by the Lord. Instances of fathers or mothers who have required from their children a violation of any one of God's commandments are very rare. Even those who themselves do not hesitate to transgress are seldom so abandoned as even to desire their children to follow their example.

1. *Obey your parents in all things; not in those which are easy and pleasant merely, but in those which are unpleasant and diffi-*

cult. To go on a long errand in the dark and in the cold; to do it when you can see no reason why it may not just as well be put off till to-morrow, is as much a duty, when your father or mother so directs, as it would be to obey the command to make yourself ready to go on a party of pleasure to which you have been long looking forward with eager expectation.

2. *Obedience should be prompt and unquestioning.* A parent is under no obligation to give a reason for any duty he may require; and if a reason be given, it is a matter of no consequence whether it be satisfactory in the judgment of the child or not. His duty is to obey—not to ask questions. Some children are always troublesome in this respect. If directed to do anything, or to refrain from doing it, they do not say "I will not," but, what is almost as bad, they pester their parents by reiterating the questions Why? and What for?

3. *Obedience to parents is a duty not only when they are present, but in their absence.* Of course this is self-evident, but it is sometimes forgotten; as, for instance, when a little girl diligently studies her lesson while her mother is in the room, but shuts

her book and plays with her doll, or amuses herself in any other way, if her mother happens to be called into the parlor to see a visitor.

While Edgar knew that his father was watching him, he was very diligently trying to do a sum in the rule of three; but when he saw that his father's attention was turned in another direction, he commenced playing with himself a game of tit-tat-toe on his slate. This leads to the remark,

4. *That the probability or even the certainty of never being detected is no good reason for disobedience.* Edgar's father and the mother of the little girl just referred to would not know but what they had been diligently employed. But there is ONE who knows all about it; it is HE who gave us the command to honor our fathers and mothers, and to obey our parents in all things; HE sees us at all times and in all places, and never regards mere *eye-service* (Eph. vi, 6) with approbation.

5. *We are to obey what we know to be the wishes of our parents, whether they have given us verbal commandment to do so or not.* The two cases already referred to illustrate this point. Both of those children

knew that their parents wished them to attend to their lessons, although no specific command had been given. When they neglected those lessons because they were no longer watched, they were guilty of disobedience, and added thereto the guilt of deception, if not of hypocrisy.

Marcus was permitted to spend a part of his vacation with his aunt, who lived in a country village. While he was there great placards were one day posted about the streets, giving notice that a circus would be opened under a tent on the common. There were to be dancing, and horse-riding, and a very funny farce. Marcus was invited to go with his two cousins, both of whom were older than he. They were surprised when he said no to their invitation; but they could not help respecting him when they knew his reason. His mother had not forbidden him. Possibly she might never know anything about it. "But," said Marcus, "I don't think she would like it." That was all. So he staid at home while the rest went to the circus, and amused himself by reading a book of travels.

Questions on Lesson XXX.

1. What is the subject of this lesson?
2. What is said of professions of love and reverence?
3. Repeat the passages quoted from the New Testament.
4. Why are these passages addressed to children only?
5. What are exceptions to the obedience required?
6. What are very rare?
7. How is the duty first enforced?
8. What is said, secondly, should be the character of obedience?
9. What is a parent under no obligation to do?
10. What is said of some children?
11. What is the third remark on this subject?
12. Illustrate a little girl's forgetfulness of this.
13. Relate what is said about Edgar.
14. What is the next observation?
15. Who would know of their disobedience?
16. What is eye-service?
17. What is the fifth direction on this subject?
18. Of what besides disobedience were these children guilty?
19. Where did Marcus spend a part of his vacation?
20. What happened while he was there?
21. Why did not Marcus go to the circus?

LESSON THIRTY-FIRST.

WAR AND BLOODSHED.

The commandment immediately following that which enjoins us to honor our fathers and mothers is brief, but very comprehensive, *Thou shalt not kill.*

This law is violated by all *aggressive wars*, and such cannot be undertaken without national and individual guilt. By aggressive wars are to be understood all that are undertaken for purposes other than those of self-defense, as for the sake of acquiring what the world calls glory, for avenging an insult, for plunder, or for the acquisition of territory. Such wars are commenced and prosecuted with the avowed intention to kill, and are clearly forbidden.

The positive command, *Thou* shalt not kill, is addressed equally to every man in an army; and in an aggressive war the soldier cannot escape blood-guiltiness by pleading the number of his associates, or the orders of his commanding officer. If it be said that nations will not take this view

SOLDIERS.

of the subject, and that to do so would subject them to the charge of cowardice, the answer is, that whether men will listen or not, it is ours to set before them the laws of morality as revealed by the Creator.

By plainly setting forth the teachings of God's word, and not by concealing or attempting to neutralize it, we may expect the glorious era spoken of by the prophets to be hastened. As one out of many of these predictions, and as a sample of them all, commit to memory this from the evangelical prophet: *They shall turn their swords into plowshares and their spears into pruning hooks; nation shall not lift up sword against nation, neither shall they learn war any more.* Isa. ii, 4.

A nation has a right to defend itself against foreign invasion, and to put down domestic rebellion. In either of these cases the guilt of violating the commandment now under consideration is incurred by the aggressor. The right and the duty to repel foreign invasion inheres in the very fact that God is the source of all government and that it is HE who is the founder of nations. *There is no power but of God,* says the apostle. *The powers that be,* that is, the authority of government in nations, *are ordained of God. Whosoever, therefore, resisteth the power resisteth the ordinance of God, and they that resist shall receive to themselves damnation.* Romans xiii, 1, 2.

Equally emphatic is the apostle's language with reference to domestic rebellion, and the right and duty of a government to suppress it, even by the use of the sword. *Rulers are not a terror to good works, but to the evil. . . . If thou do that which is evil be afraid, for he beareth not the sword in vain; for he is the minister of God, a revenger to execute wrath upon him that doeth evil.* Romans xiii, 3, 4.

The exceptions to the broad and unqualified command, Thou shalt not kill, can only be such as are made by Him who gave it. These refer first to animals, secondly to human beings.

After the deluge God gave to Noah and his descendants permission to kill animals for food: *Every moving thing that liveth shall be meat for you,* (Gen. ix, 3;) and in the vision seen by the apostle Peter he was directed *to kill and eat of four-footed beasts of the earth, and wild beasts, and creeping things, and fowls of the air.* Acts x, 12, 13.

Permission has also been given to kill animals that are hostile and dangerous to man, among which may be included the different kinds of noxious and destructive vermin. The apostle speaks of *natural brute beasts made to be taken and destroyed*, (2 Peter ii, 12,) and Paul shook off into the fire a viper that had fastened on his hand. Acts xxviii, 3–5.

As to human life, there is but one thing that specifically warrants its destruction. It is the crime of murder, and the warrant is found in the command given to Noah and, as is generally believed, through him to all people: *Whoso sheddeth man's blood by man shall his blood be shed.* Gen. ix, 6. It is not universally agreed whether this language is to be understood as a positive command or only as a prediction.

The weight of argument seems to be in favor of considering it as a command. Admitting it to be so, for no other crime is society warranted in taking human life; and even in the case of deliberate murder, the penalty is not to be inflicted save by the regular course of judicial proceedings. He who kills a murderer, save as the executioner of the law, is himself a murderer.

Questions on Lesson XXXI.

1. What is the sixth commandment?
2. How is this command violated?
3. What are to be understood by aggressive wars?
4. To whom is the command addressed?
5. Does the number of his associates or the order of his commanding officer justify a soldier in shedding blood?
6. How may we expect to hasten the time foretold by the prophets?
7. What is the prediction on this subject?
8. What has a nation the right to do?
9. What is said of domestic rebellion?
10. In these cases on whom rests the guilt of violating this commandment?
11. By what argument is proved the right of repelling foreign invasion?
12. Repeat Romans xiii, 1, 2.
13. What is said of the apostle's language with reference to domestic rebellion?
14. Repeat the passage quoted.
15. Who has the right to make exceptions to this broad command?
16. To what do the exceptions made by him refer?
17. What permission did God give to Noah?
18. What was the direction to Peter in the vision, Acts x, 12, 13?
19. What other animals may be killed?
20. What warrants the destruction of human life?
21. Can you quote Genesis ix, 6?
22. How only is the penalty to be inflicted?

LESSON THIRTY-SECOND.

FIGHTING, DUELING, SUICIDE.

As in the violation of other commandments there are degrees of guilt, some being more and others less heinous, so it is with transgressions of the law which says *Thou shalt not kill.* To take the life of a human being in cold blood, with malice aforethought, which constitutes the technical crime known as murder, is undoubtedly the most grievous violation of this commandment.

Very similar, and with scarcely a shade of difference in the degree of guilt, is death inflicted in a combat between two individuals. He who kills his antagonist in a duel is a murderer, with guilt upon his soul sometimes even blacker than that which is expiated on the gallows.

Several circumstances heighten the guilt of the duelist. In the first place he is generally a man of more intelligence and education than those who commit the crime legally known as murder. Then the duelist goes calmly and deliberately about his bloody work. He has time, which is not always the case with ordinary murderers, for deliberation and reflection. Generally he prepares himself for his task by practice. He fires at a mark to acquire calmness of nerve and accuracy of eye. He determines to kill or be killed, and makes his will. The fact that he risks being killed himself does not in any degree palliate, but rather enhances his criminality. He has as little right to throw away his own life as to take that of another.

This leads to the remark that *suicide* is also a grievous violation of this law. In most cases he who voluntarily takes his own life not only kills his body, but murders his soul. It is difficult to conceive how surviving friends can have any hope for the future destiny of him who has rushed unbidden into the presence of his Maker. Of the traitor Judas we are told that after hanging himself he went *to his own place,* (Acts i, 25,) which cannot be supposed to mean the abode of the pure in heart, in the home of the blessed.

To do anything which may cause the death of others is a violation of this commandment. A little boy only ten years of age, who lived in the country, was sent of an errand one Saturday afternoon. On his way he had to cross a railroad, in doing which he saw that some malicious person had placed a large bar of iron on the track. It was just at a curve, which would render it impossible for the engineer to see it. After trying in vain to remove it, the little fellow ran on some distance, and presently a large train of cars, with several hundred passengers, made its appearance. Standing in the middle of the road and waving his hat, he succeeded in stopping them; and the passengers, when they saw the danger they had escaped, were loud in his praise, and made him a handsome present. The miscreant who placed that bar of iron upon the track was just as guilty as he would have been if his design had succeeded, and a terrible loss of life had ensued. His motive was to kill, and, as we saw in a former lesson, the motive is always to be taken into the account when the guilt of an act is estimated.

To wound or maim an individual, although death do not immediately ensue, is also forbidden by this law. The crime is not so heinous as if life were taken, and yet there may be circumstances connected with the act that make it as bad as murder. In a fight between two men which lasted several hours, and an account of which was published in the papers, the one at length knocked the other down. It was at first supposed that he was killed. He lay apparently senseless for a long time, and although consciousness returned, he never fully recovered from the effects of the blow. He was an invalid for several months, and then died. Human law winked at the offense, but in the eye of Heaven that man was murdered.

So in the case of a fight between two boys at a boarding-school; the surgeon declared that if a blow struck by one of them had been half an inch more to the left death would have been the consequence. How dreadful to both boys, to their parents and friends, and brothers and sisters, if that blow *had* been fatal. No special credit is due to him who struck that blow for the half inch which made all the difference between death and a wound which was healed in a few weeks. It might have been otherwise; and the mere allusion to it, one would think, ought to be sufficient to deter others from allowing their angry passions so to overcome them as to lead them into such fearful possibilities.

Questions on Lesson XXXII.

1. In what respect does the sixth commandment resemble the others?
2. What constitutes the crime known as murder?
3. What is said of murder?
4. What very nearly resembles murder?
5. What heightens the guilt of the duelist?
6. How does he go about his bloody work?
7. How does he generally prepare himself for it?
8. What is said of the fact that the duelist risks his own life?
9. What is said of suicide?
10. Of what is the suicide generally guilty?
11. What is the probability of his future destiny?
12. Whither is Judas said to have gone at his death?
13. What do you suppose that means?
14. Mention another violation of this commandment.
15. How is this illustrated?
16. What is said of him who placed the impediment on the track?
17. What else is forbidden by this law?
18. What may circumstances make this act?
19. What is the illustration?
20. What about the fight at a boarding-school?
21. What effect ought this to produce?

LESSON THIRTY-THIRD.

HATRED—MURDER.

In speaking of the first murderer, Cain, who slew his brother because the works of Abel were righteous and his own works were evil, the beloved disciple makes this fearful declaration: *Whoso hateth his brother is a murderer.* 1 John iii, 15.

By *brother* he means any human being, and by thus speaking of hatred he intends most forcibly to warn us against the indulgence of this feeling toward a fellow-creature.

It is not that he who hates another has actually taken away his life, nor that he who indulges this feeling certainly will shed blood. There are many things that may restrain him, as the reproaches of conscience, a want of opportunity, or the fear of being found out. Yet, though he should be restrained by either or by all of these considerations, he who hates his fellow-creature is, in the sight of God, a murderer; for HE looketh upon the heart; and the crime lies not in the outward act so much as in the disposition of the soul and its intentions and purposes.

This being the case, it becomes us to guard against the first symptoms of hatred, and, if possible, to seek out and destroy the causes from which it may arise.

One of these causes, and perhaps the most common, is *envy*.

Envy led on Cain first to hate and then to kill his brother. Envy is with great frequency denounced in the Scriptures. Solomon says it *is the rottenness of the bones*. Prov. xiv, 30. The Apostle Paul classes it with *covetousness, maliciousness, and murder*. Rom. i, 29. The brothers of Joseph first envied and then hated the little fellow for whom his father had made a coat of many colors. Then they sold him for a slave, and almost broke the heart of their father by pretending that a wild beast had devoured him. Gen. xxxvii.

Envy needs to be the more carefully watched against because it is very nearly allied to an affection of the heart which, when not carried to excess, is right and proper. One of the coarsehand copies sometimes given by the teacher of penmanship is, "Emulation is laudable." So it is, within certain limits.

Horace and Robert were among the best scholars in the school. They were both good boys and loved each other dearly. The examining committee, which visited the school twice a year, had proposed to give a very valuable prize to the boy who should give evidence of the best scholarship. Long before the time for awarding the premium it was pretty well known that it would be won either by Robert or Horace. The other scholars had given up the struggle, and watched with great earnestness the strife between the two competitors. Some favored one, some favored the other.

Up to a certain point the emulation between the two boys was proper, but as the day approached which was to decide the contest the struggle became more earnest and more selfish. At first they used to go to each other's house and study together. That was soon given up, and in a little while neither would give the other the least assistance. Then one would take unfair advantage of the other in their recitations, and very soon all the scholars could see that the rivals did not love each other as they once did.

It had been better for them both if no

prize had been offered, for emulation had now ripened into jealousy, and neither could bear to hear the other well-spoken of by the teacher or by any one else.

Worse than this; when it became evident, as it did a week before the examination, that Robert was ahead and would certainly get the prize, envy took full possession of Horace, and, as it almost always does, envy ripened into hatred, and his hatred soon had an opportunity to show itself.

Not like Cain did Horace actually take life, but, seizing the opportunity one dark night, as he watched him going of an errand, he hurled a stone at Robert's head, which might have killed him, but only inflicted a severe wound. Poor Robert never found out who did it, and no eye but that of God saw the act; and with him we must leave it to estimate the guilt incurred.

Hatred sometimes springs from *a real or fancied injury.* It is a matter of little consequence whether the injury has really been done or whether it is only suspected. In either case it is equally unjustifiable, equally injurious to him who indulges the malevolent feeling, and equally abhorrent in the eyes of God.

And once more, so perverse is human nature, and so corrupt is the human heart, that a feeling of hatred is indulged when *no reason whatever can be assigned for it.* The Son of God said of those who thirsted for his blood, and who were about to put him to death, *They hated me without cause.* John xv, 25.

So, too, you may have read in profane history of him who was surnamed the Just. His countrymen sent him into banishment, and one of the rabble who, voted for that cruel deed, when asked why he so hated Aristides, had no better reply to make than that he was tired of hearing him continually called the Just.

Questions on Lesson XXXIII.

1. What fearful declaration is first alluded to in this lesson?
2. Whom does the apostle mean by brother?
3. What does he intend by thus speaking of hatred?
4. What is not the apostle's meaning?
5. What may restrain him who hates from actual murder?
6. In whose sight is he who hates his brother a murderer?

7. What inference is drawn from this fact?
8. What is the most common cause of hatred?
9. Repeat what Solomon says about envy.
10. With what vices does St. Paul class it?
11. Can you relate the outline of the story of Joseph?
12. To what affection is envy nearly allied?
13. What is said of emulation?
14. What is said of Horace and Robert?
15. What of their emulation up to a certain point?
16. As the day approached what did the contest become?
17. What did the scholars perceive?
18. What had been better for them both?
19. When envy took possession of Horace what soon followed?
20. How did he show his hatred?
21. What source of hatred is next mentioned?
22. What is said of hatred arising from this source?
23. What does Christ say of himself in John xv; 25?
24. What is said about Aristides?

LESSON THIRTY-FOURTH.

CRUELTY TO ANIMALS.

Thus far, in considering violations of the sixth commandment, our attention has been confined to human beings. But the law is broad and unqualified. It forbids killing,

A CRUEL BOY.

or the taking of animal life, except in those cases and under those circumstances which have been already specified. True, the life of a man is of vastly more importance than the life of a dumb animal; but it by no means follows that the life of a dumb animal is of no importance. God does not so regard it, and man has no right to set up his opinion against that of his Maker.

Ye are of more value than many sparrows. Matt. x, 31. Certainly ye are. In the days of the Saviour five of them were sold for two farthings, and they are probably worth no more now; and yet *not one of them is forgotten before God.* Luke xii, 6.

By the Levitical law the raven was deemed an unclean bird, (Lev. xi, 15,) yet frequent reference is made to God's providential care for him. Job xxxviii, 41; Psalm cxlvii, 9; Luke xii, 24. Of the innumerable inhabitants of the ocean the psalmist says they all wait upon HIM who *giveth them their meat in due season.* Psalm civ, 27.

The ox and the ass were deemed worthy of a place in one of the ten commandments. Exod. xx, 17. In another chapter (xxiii, 17) God gives as one reason for the establishment of a weekly Sabbath, *that thine ox and thine ass may rest.* On two different occasions (1 Cor. ix, 9, and 1 Tim. v, 18) the Apostle Paul quotes God's merciful recognition of the laboring beast in his toils for the benefit of man. *Thou shalt not muzzle the ox when he treadeth out the corn.* Deut. xxv, 4.

From these general principles we deduce several practical inferences.

1. Inasmuch as all animals are our fellow-creatures, called into being by the same God to whom we are indebted for our existence, we can have no right to abuse them, and no right to use them in any other manner than our Creator permits and sanctions.

2. For purposes of food, inasmuch as we have express permission to make the flesh

of beasts, of birds, and of fish a part of our diet, we may put them to death. Conscience and Scripture alike teach that in so doing we should inflict as little pain as possible. The poet says:

> The poor beetle that we tread upon
> In corporal sufferance feels a pang as great
> As when a giant dies.—SHAKSPEARE.

This may possibly be an exaggeration, although we cannot prove that it is. Brutes are so unlike ourselves that we can institute no comparison between their nature and our own; yet is it most certain that they are keenly susceptible of pain, although they seldom make any outcry.

3. The same remark applies to noxious animals and vermin. They may be put to death because we have the Creator's sanction for their destruction, and our own lives, in some instances, may be endangered if they are permitted to live. Even with regard to them, however, there is no warrant for cruelty or the infliction of unnecessary pain. A rattlesnake is a very venomous reptile. It may be killed whenever met with; but it would be wrong to torture it, or to prolong its agony.

4. There are many animals which we have no right to destroy. They are not included in either of the divisions. They are not injurious to man, and they are not necessary for food. To them applies the command, Thou shalt not kill: to harmless birds, for instance, that no one pretends to want for food; to beautiful butterflies that God made to enjoy a short summer's life, and to little fishes that, in sport, are drawn out of the water by a torturing hook to die. Children frequently do these things without thinking; but that is no excuse. They ought to think. The poet Cowper is very severe upon this want of thought, even with reference to crawling reptiles:

> I would not enter on my list of friends
> (Though graced with polished manners and fine sense,
> Yet wanting sensibility) the man
> Who needlessly sets foot upon a worm.

5. Finally, the disposition of heart that lies at the bottom of all these violations of the commandment with reference to animals and to human beings, is *cruelty*. Indulging in a cruel disposition, the child is led on from the wanton destruction of insects, step by step, to the higher degrees of guilt. A man who was recently hung for an atrocious

murder traced back his career of guilt to the days of his childhood, when, unchecked, he indulged and fostered the cruelty of his disposition by torturing innocent dumb animals. The remedy is in early life to cultivate feelings of tenderness and compassion, and ever to remember that Jesus has pronounced a *blessing upon the merciful, for they shall obtain mercy.* Matt. v, 7.

Questions on Lesson XXXIV.

1. What is the subject of this lesson?
2. What is said of this law?
3. Does God regard the lives of dumb animals?
4. What is said in Matt. x, 31?
5. What is said of sparrows in Luke xii, 6?
6. What is the raven considered by the Levitical law?
7. Quote some passages which show God's care for ravens.
8. What is said of the fishes in the sea, Psa. civ, 27?
9. In which commandment are the ox and the ass mentioned?
10. What is stated in Exod. xxiii, 17, as one reason for a weekly Sabbath?
11. What is written in Deut. xxv, 4?
12. In what books of the New Testament is this passage referred to?

13. What is the first inference drawn from these principles?
14. In putting dumb animals to death what should we do?
15. What is said of the sentiment of the poet?
16. Why may we put noxious animals to death?
17. In putting them to death what may we not do?
18. What is said of the rattlesnake?
19. What kinds of animals are we forbidden to kill?
20. What does Cowper say of thoughtless cruelty?
21. What is the disposition of heart that leads to these violations of the commandment?
22. What is said of a man recently hung?
23. What should we cultivate?
24. What says Jesus Christ in Matt. v, 7?

LESSON THIRTY-FIFTH.

HONESTY.

To be honest in all our dealings is enjoined equally by divine and by human laws. A very large portion of the duties of those who make and of those who execute the laws of the land is occupied in enacting and enforcing penalties for dishonesty. Of the inmates of penitentiaries and prisons the greater number have been guilty of some species of fraud, or of some attempt to appropriate to themselves the property of others. The variety of methods by which this is done is almost infinite; and human ingenuity seems to be tasked to its uttermost to devise new modes of swindling, and of obtaining the property of others by false pretenses.

By the laws of the land degrees of guilt are graduated and penalties affixed to all kinds of discovered dishonesty, from that of the public defaulter, whose rascality is dignified by being called a breach of trust, to the pickpocket or common thief, whose paltry gains are branded as larceny, grand or petit, according to the amount stolen.

But there is a vast amount of dishonesty that is never made known in this world, and a great deal for which human laws have no punishment, but which are none the less condemned by conscience and the revealed will of God. *He that is unjust in the least,* says Christ, *is unjust also in much.* Luke xvi, 10. By this he does not mean to teach us that all acts of injustice are equally heinous in his sight. That is not the case. In *his* sight there are degrees of guilt in dishonest actions, but elements enter into his reckoning of which men make no account.

As, for instance, the motive by which a man is actuated. Human tribunals cannot take this into consideration. God always does. Of two store-keepers each of whom offers for sale damaged articles at a high price, the one may have disposed of but a few, the other of a great many. The guilt of the latter, according to man's judgment, is much the greater; not so in the sight of Heaven. The intention of each was to defraud the ignorant, and they both did so to the extent of their opportunity. Hence, guilt is not to be estimated by its gain. Among men it seems to be necessary that the degree of criminality should be thus measured. The value of things stolen decides the amount of punishment inflicted by an earthly court; but even with our limited capacities we can see that it will not be so at that higher tribunal where all things will be made known, and to which we are all amenable. There may be just as much guilt in stealing a pocketbook which proves to be empty as there would have been had it contained a thousand dollars.

Nor, again, are we to infer that those who commit what the world deems little acts of injustice do actually commit greater, for they are restrained sometimes by public opinion. Many who do not fear God regard man, and are restrained by that regard. A merchant who will not hesitate to cheat a little, by false weights and measures, will not venture to forge a check in the name of his neighbor. To be found out in so doing would ruin him, and it is too great a risk to run; but it is more than probable that his petty acts of dishonesty will never be discovered; and if they are, that the world will look upon them with leniency, and that they will not bring him to the bar of public justice. Evidently this man is none the more entitled to be called honest because he is restrained from grosser acts of fraud by the fear of being found out, than he would be if that fear were taken away and he were to carry into practice the desire of his heart.

It has been said that he who is only legally honest, that is, only so honest as to keep out of the reach of the laws of the land, is a great rascal. The boundary between honesty and dishonesty is a straight line, and leaves on the wrong side of it every act of injustice and wrong-doing, however trivial in human estimation, and however sanctioned by the customs of society. He who takes one step across that line is as really on the other side of it as he who has taken two, ten, or a thousand. Such is the meaning of the Saviour's teaching: *He that is unjust in the least is unjust also in much.*

QUESTIONS ON LESSON XXXV.

1. What is enjoined equally by divine and by human laws?
2. What occupies a large part of the time of legislators and executive officers?
3. What is said of the inmates of prisons and penitentiaries?
4. For what purpose is man's ingenuity exerted?
5. What is done by the laws of the land?
6. What is larceny?
7. What is said of a vast amount of dishonesty?
8. What saying of Jesus Christ is quoted?
9. Are all acts of injustice equally heinous in his sight?
10. What enters into the reckoning, of which man makes no account?
11. What is the illustration from two store-keepers?
12. Wherein were they both alike?
13. What is said of the gain of dishonesty?
14. What decides the amount of punishment inflicted by an earthly tribunal?
15. What is said of an empty pocket-book?

16. What is said of those who commit little acts of injustice?
17. By what are many restrained who do not fear God?
18. What is the illustration?
19. If he should commit a forgery, what would probably be the result?
20. What has been said of him who is only legally honest?
21. What is the boundary between honesty and dishonesty?
22. What is said of him who steps across that line?

LESSON THIRTY-SIXTH.

DISHONESTY.

THE commandment which enjoins honesty is brief and comprehensive: *Thou shalt not steal.* Exod. xx, 15. To steal is to take the property of another without his consent. The amount taken, as we saw in the last lesson, is not an essential part of the action. It is as really an act of theft to steal an apple as to steal a dollar. He that would do the former would do the latter under favorable circumstances; that is, he would do it if it were not for fear of being detected; or if, when detected, he could persuade himself that no evil consequences would follow, that he would not lose his good name, nor forfeit the respect of his associates.

No exception is made as respects those from whom property is taken. It is theft to steal from parents no less than it is to steal from strangers. *Whoso robbeth his father or his mother, and saith it is no transgression, the same is the companion of a destroyer* [or *a murderer*.] Prov. xxviii, 24. If a boy on his return from an errand gives his mother but one half of the change that he received from the store-keeper, that boy is guilty of theft just as really as if he had stolen that money from a stranger or taken it out of the store-keeper's drawer.

When Horatio left home and went to a boarding-school several hundred miles distant, his father intrusted him with ten silver dollars, to be used, if necessary, in paying any expenses that might arise. At that school the larger boys had formed themselves into a ball club, and were in the habit, with the approbation of their teacher, of playing several times a week. Horatio was invited to join the club. The entrance fee which each paid when admitted was fifty cents. "I shall have to write home first," said Horatio, and ask consent of my father." "Why no," replied his room-mate; "your father gave you that money, and it is yours to do what you like with it." This was a view of the case which would have satisfied many boys, but Horatio replied: "True, father gave me the money; but he gave it to me for the purpose of paying necessary expenses. I might buy books with it, or clothes, or pay for medicine if I were sick; but to pay the fee for joining a club did not enter into his calculation." So he wrote to his father about it, and did not unite with the club until he received an answer to his letter. Horatio did right, and even those boys who had tried to persuade him to do otherwise could not help seeing that his conduct was right and proper.

In the commandment no exception is made for peculiar circumstances, or for the force of temptation. Suppose your mother is sick, and that she is very anxious to taste a ripe peach. A churlish neighbor has a tree full of them, but will neither sell nor give you one. You will not be justified in stealing, although you may have a fine opportunity of doing so without detection, and the owner will not miss what you take.

The question has been sometimes asked if a hungry man might not steal bread to appease the cravings of appetite; to which the answer must also be in the negative, although doubtless in the judgment of Heaven the man's hunger may be, in some sense, a palliation of his guilt.

To depreciate the value of another's property, without taking it entirely from him, is a species of dishonesty that is very frequently practiced. How common a thing it is to borrow a book, and return it torn, or unnecessarily soiled, perhaps with a picture abstracted from it; and how dishonest such conduct is! To abuse anything borrowed from another, or to use it in any way in which we would not use our own property, is none the less a violation of common honesty because it is done thoughtlessly, without the willful intention of doing wrong.

There is also a great deal of thoughtless dishonesty which arises from idleness and a love of mischief combined. In some large schools you can scarcely find a desk or a bench that has not been cut and hacked by idle and dishonest school-boys. So also in the surrounding fences and outhouses a spirit of mischief and thoughtless destruction is everywhere apparent. The same thing is seen occasionally even in the house of God. The walls are disfigured by charcoal and black lead pencils, and not unfrequently the perpetrator of such acts scrawls his own name, as if glorying in his shame, and anxious that everybody should know to whom belongs the guilt of such disgraceful conduct. Initiated in these courses at school, when boys grow up to be men they indulge in the same practices. There is scarcely a public building in the land but what is hacked, and defaced, and disfigured to a greater or less degree. Avoid all such mean and dishonest conduct.

Questions on Lesson XXXVI.

1. What is the commandment that enjoins honesty?
2. How do you define stealing?
3. What is not an essential part of the action?
4. Under what circumstances would he who steals an apple steal a dollar?

5. Is exception made as to those from whom property is taken?
6. What does Solomon say on the subject?
7. Give the illustration of a boy sent on an errand.
8. Tell in your own language the story of Horatio.
9. What do you think of Horatio's conduct in this matter?
10. For what does the commandment make no exception?
11. What is the illustration?
12. What of stealing bread to appease hunger?
13. What species of dishonesty is next mentioned?
14. How is this illustrated?
15. What is said of abusing things borrowed?
16. From what does a great deal of thoughtless dishonesty arise?
17. What may be found in some large school-rooms?
18. What are the boys called who do these things?
19. Where else is this spirit of mischief seen?
20. How are churches sometimes disfigured?
21. What does the perpetrator of such acts frequently do?
22. When such boys grow up to be men what do they frequently do?
23. What is said of public buildings?

LESSON THIRTY-SEVENTH.

HONESTY IN LITTLE THINGS.

1. *Borrowing without a probability of paying* is one of the things forbidden by the General Rules of the Church. It is forbidden because it has in it the elements of dishonesty. It is not exactly stealing, and is frequently practiced by those who would shudder at the thought of fraudently appropriating to themselves the property of another. It cannot be done without deception. Those who borrow always profess the intention to repay; else, of course, no one would be found willing to lend.

2. Again: *The law of honesty requires that debts be paid when due, and in the manner promised.* If I borrow money, or anything else, for a week, I am under the most sacred obligation to make payment at the end of that time. A merchant or tradesman may frequently be seen hurrying to the bank to pay a note. This note is nothing but a promise to pay a certain sum at a certain time. That time has arrived, and

hence the anxiety to discharge the debt. The fact that a note was given does not increase the obligation. The word of an honest man ought to be regarded just as binding as his written promise; and although the law might not take hold of him for not keeping his word, yet he who violates a verbal promise forfeits his reputation as an honest man.

There was a loud rap at the door one stormy Saturday night. It was raining very hard, as it had been most of the day. We were all surprised that any one should call upon us on such an evening. It was a neighbor who lived nearly a mile off, who had borrowed a book with the promise to return it by the end of the week. Very carefully he had wrapped it up in stiff brown paper, and as carefully he had carried it under his coat to keep it from being soiled by the rain. Many persons would have thought the heavy shower a sufficient excuse for not returning the book at the promised time, while a storm of much greater severity would not have been deemed a good reason for neglecting to pay a note in the bank. He who returned the book at such inconvenience to himself had the satisfaction of feeling that he had kept his word, and the assurance that he might call again and ask to borrow without fear of a refusal.

3. *To conceal defects in an article we wish to sell or give in exchange for something else is dishonest.* Here, again, the law of Christian morals is in advance of the laws of the land, which, according to the Latin proverb, (*Caveat emptor*, Let the buyer look out for himself,) throw upon the purchaser the duty of examining for himself, and leave him no redress for not discovering flaws or other defects that have been carefully concealed. "I did not warrant him sound," said the farmer who had sold a spavined horse which the purchaser wished to return. No, he did not say, in so many words, I warrant the animal; but he very well knew at the time he made the sale that the purchaser was deceived, and that *he* was deceiving him.

4. Of the same moral character is the act of *undervaluing the property of another which we desire to obtain.* This species of dishonesty was common in the days of Solomon. He refers to it in the book of Proverbs: *It is naught, it is naught, saith the*

buyer; but when he is gone his way then he boasteth. Prov. xx, 14. He boasteth of the good bargain he has made by pretending to the seller that the article was of little value; he boasteth, in a word, of having cheated him. So common is this practice at the present day that many store-keepers uniformly ask a higher price for their goods than they are willing to take. They expect to be "beat down," as the phrase is; and they are willing to allow their customers to boast of their bargains when, in reality, they have paid for articles purchased quite as much as they were worth.

5. *Honesty will not permit advantage to be taken of another's ignorance or carelessness even in the smallest matters.* In making change for a dollar the grocer gave a boy ten cents too much. He ought to have returned it immediately. He had no more right to keep it than if he had stolen it. The plea that the grocer gave him that ten cents is absurd and false.

In one of the city rail-cars the other day a little girl handed the conductor six cents. He looked at her a moment, and seeing that she was not ten years of age told her the fare was but three cents. "I know it," said she; "but when I rode down yesterday you forgot to ask for my money, so now I pay you for both rides." This was nothing more than right; but the conductor looked as if such instances of common honesty were not frequent in his experience.

Questions on Lesson XXXVII.

1. What is first noticed in this lesson?
2. Why is it forbidden?
3. By whom is it frequently practiced?
4. What do those who borrow always profess?
5. What is next said to be required by the law of honesty?
6. What may merchants and tradesmen be frequently seen doing?
7. What is a note?
8. What is said of the word of an honest man?
9. How may a man forfeit his reputation for honesty?
10. Relate the story about the borrowed book?
11. What satisfaction had he who restored the book?
12. What act of dishonesty is next mentioned?
13. How does Christian morality compare with the laws of the land in this respect?
14. What is the Latin proverb and its interpretation?
15. What conduct of the farmer is used in illustration?
16. What is the dishonesty next mentioned?
17. What is the quotation from Proverbs?
18. Explain it.

19. What shows this to be a common practice?
20. What do many store-keepers expect?
21. What is next said of honesty?
22. Relate the illustration from the case of the grocer and the boy.
23. Tell us about the little girl in the railcar.

LESSON THIRTY-EIGHTH.

GAMBLING.

Of that species of dishonesty which is known by the general name of *gambling* there are many varieties. They are all alike in the one distinguishing feature that their votaries seek to obtain the property of others without rendering an equivalent for it.

Gaming houses are to be found in all large cities. In some they are regularly licensed by the government. Of course the proprietors amass the wealth which is lost by those who visit them; and although occasionally an individual may win a trifle, yet the great majority always lose, and sometimes so largely as to cause poverty, madness, and suicide.

The practice of *betting* is not confined to

gaming houses. On the speed of two horses or two ships, on the truth or falsity of any statement, or on any future contingency whatever, men will be found anxious to stake a sum of money on condition that another will risk a similar amount. Even little boys readily imbibe the habit, and offer bets sometimes without a thought that in so doing they are gambling, and that gambling is wicked.

Lotteries are near akin to gaming houses, and, in some respects, even worse in their evil effects. Those who buy tickets do so in the hope that by the outlay of a little money they shall gain a great deal. They who have the management of lotteries, on the other hand, are careful to arrange the blanks and prizes so that the winners shall be very few, the losers many. This, for the most part, is well known to those who buy the tickets; but there is something so fascinating to many minds in the idea of obtaining money by what is called *luck* rather than by honest industry, that wherever lotteries are tolerated persons will be found willing and anxious to risk the little they have in the hope of gaining more.

It does not at all lessen the iniquity of

lotteries that they are licensed by some civil governments, nor is the disgraceful fact that Christian Churches have established and patronized them any argument in their favor. It may be admitted that the profits arising from the sale of tickets have been applied to charitable and religious purposes; but it will still be true that we are not justifiable in doing evil, even though good may result from it. Inducing people to lay out their money in the purchase of lottery tickets is doing evil just as surely as inducing them to gamble in any other way.

As a general thing, Protestant Churches at the present day would not sanction a lottery for any purposes, however laudable. In some instances, from a want of thought probably, objectionable practices have crept into what are known as *church fairs*. To charge greatly more than an article is worth, because the profits are for a benevolent object, seems hardly consistent with strict integrity. To levy a tax on visitors in the guise of postage for a sham letter may be a good joke, but has in it a savor of dishonesty. The grab bag is nothing but a lottery on a paltry scale; and those who buy shares in a large cake, with the hope of obtaining the piece with a gold ring in it, are perhaps not aware that they are actually gambling.

These, it will be said, are small matters. In a certain sense they are; but the Saviour laid down the principle, *He that is unjust in the least is unjust also in much*, to teach us not to regard as trivial any deviation from the straight path of integrity and uprightness. Besides, indulging in what are deemed little sins leads to the commission of such as are more heinous; and he who would avoid the name and the fate of a dishonest gambler must not allow little temptations to beguile him into wrong-doing.

Crazy Josh, as he is called, is a harmless, apparently half-witted old man. He depends on charity for his daily bread. He was an only child, and his parents were rich. They idolized this boy, and allowed him to have his own way in almost everything. When a lad he exhibited a fondness for gambling, which, being indulged, led him from shooting marbles with his schoolmates to pitching pennies with all the bad boys of the village. He almost always lost, for he was easily cheated. In succession, as he grew older, he began to play with dice, and dominoes, and cards. He attended horse-races and made bets, and was well known in what were called the sporting circles. At the death of his father, which took place when Joshua was one-and-twenty, he came into possession of a large amount of property, which he lost in a very few years at the gaming table. Then for a while he was dependent on his mother. She had just enough to provide comfortably for her wants. By his earnest and repeated entreaties the old lady, at a time when she was enfeebled by disease, was induced to put all her property into his hands. For a while he kept his resolution not to risk it at the gaming table. But a race between two celebrated horses was a temptation too strong for him. He bet all he was worth on his favorite, in the confident expectation of doubling his money. His favorite was beaten, and he was ruined. The shock was too much for his mother. She took to her bed and died, and was indebted to charitable neighbors for a coffin and a grave. Josh, turned from house and home, a wandering outcast, apparently bereft of his senses, gets an occasional meal from those who knew him in his prosperous days, and is glad, when these retreats fail him, to seek shelter and food in the alms-house, a living monument of the folly of gambling, and a warning to beware of the first steps that lead thither.

Questions on Lesson XXXVIII.

1. What is said of gambling?
2. In what are all kinds of gambling alike?
3. What is said of gaming houses?
4. Who amass the money that is lost at gaming houses?
5. What sometimes follows losses by gambling?
6. What is said of betting?
7. What kind of gambling is next mentioned?
8. Why do persons buy tickets?
9. How are the blanks and prizes arranged?
10. Does a knowledge of this fact prevent the purchase of tickets?
11. What fascinates the purchasers?
12. What does not lessen the iniquity of lotteries?
13. What disgraceful fact is mentioned?
14. But suppose the profits are applied to religious purposes?
15. What have crept into church fairs?
16. What is hardly consistent with strict integrity?
17. What has in it a savor of dishonesty?
18. What is a lottery on a paltry scale?
19. What is said of the cake with a gold ring in it?
20. What principle of the Saviour's is quoted?

21. What was that intended to teach us?
22. To what does indulging in little sins lead?
23. Relate in your own language the history of crazy Josh.

LESSON THIRTY-NINTH.

THIRD QUARTERLY REVISION.

In this review of the studies of the last three months the questions are confined to the lessons from the twenty-seventh to the thirty-eighth. The scholar, however, it is hoped, will be able also to answer any question founded upon the former part of the volume that may be asked by the teacher.

1. What were the names of the three Hebrews referred to in the twenty-seventh lesson?
2. Give in your own language an outline of their history as found in the book of Daniel.
3. Why do we say they did right in disobeying the king?
4. Repeat the illustration taken from the farmer and his field of wheat.

5. State the case of Mary and her lesson in geography.
6. What questions may be decided by expediency?
7. Relate briefly the history of Daniel.
8. Wherein is the conduct of Peter and John, as found in the fourth chapter of Acts, similar to that of Daniel?
9. What proposition do these illustrations establish?
10. What is the ground of total abstinence from intoxicating liquors?
11. What do you understand by the saying that two duties can never clash?
12. Repeat the commandment with promise.
13. What place does that command occupy in the decalogue?
14. How does that commandment apply to those children whose fathers and mothers are dead?
15. Can you quote a passage from the Bible in which the mother is placed before the father?
16. On what ground is placed the duty to honor our parents?
17. What are included in the duty to honor our parents?
18. What is the most essential part of the

honor due from children to their parents?

19. Repeat the ninth verse of the twelfth chapter of Hebrews.
20. How is the command to obey our parents in all things, to be understood?
21. Can we ever be said to obey our parents when they have given us no command?
22. Relate what is said of Marcus in lesson thirtieth?
23. What command is violated by aggressive wars?
24. What is said of the guilt of a soldier in an aggressive war?
25. Repeat Isaiah ii, 4.
26. In what two instances is a nation justified in going to war?
27. Where in the Bible do we find permission to kill animals for food?
28. Where is found the command to put murderers to death?
29. What is the most grievous violation of the sixth commandment?
30. What is said of the guilt of the duelist?
31. Name the several circumstances which heighten the guilt of the duelist.

32. What is said of the friends of him who commits suicide?
33. Name some other things besides the taking of life that are forbidden by the sixth commandment.
34. Repeat 1 John iii, 15, and explain it.
35. What feeling caused Cain to kill his brother?
36. Relate in your own language the story of Robert and Horace.
37. On what ground is cruelty to animals forbidden?
38. What authority have we for using animals for food?
39. Can you prove that God feeds fishes in the sea?
40. What is the rascality of a public defaulter sometimes called?
41. Repeat what Christ says in Luke xvi, 10, and explain it.
42. What is said of stealing from parents in Prov. xxviii, 24?
43. Relate the circumstances in the case of Horatio at the boarding-school.
44. Which commandment is violated by willfully injuring another's property?
45. But if it is done thoughtlessly is it less a violation of honesty?

46. Where is "borrowing without a probability of paying" expressly forbidden?
47. Does giving a note for borrowed money increase the obligation to repay that money?
48. In what respect are the laws of Christian morals in advance of the laws of the land?
49. Why do shopkeepers frequently ask more for their goods than they are willing to take?
50. What is gambling?
51. Mention some of the evils occasionally practiced at church fairs.
52. What occasioned the ruin of crazy Josh?

LESSON FORTIETH.

MARRIAGE.

MARRIAGE is a divine institution. In civilized countries it is recognized, and in some degree regulated, by the civil law. In all cases, however, the laws of the land must be subordinate to those of the Creator. No human enactment can set aside his will, or make that right which he has declared to be wrong.

In proof of the divine institution of marriage, Jesus Christ refers to the original creation of man and woman as recorded in the third chapter of Genesis. Here is the Saviour's comment and explanation upon that passage: *Have ye not read that He which made them at the beginning made them male and female, and said, For this cause shall a man leave father and mother and shall cleave to his wife, and they twain shall be one flesh. Wherefore, they are no more twain, but one flesh. What, therefore, God hath joined together let not man put asunder.* Matt. xix, 4–6. There is implied in this language:

1. That from the beginning God designed the matrimonial relation between man and woman.

2. That he not only designed it, but that he himself joins together those who are thus united.

3. That this relationship was designed for all people in all periods of time. It could not have had reference to Adam and Eve only, for they had neither father nor mother;

and here it is expressly stated that a man is to leave his parents, and by parity of reasoning a woman is also to leave hers when entering into this state; that is, that the matrimonial relationship is to supersede and to take precedence over the filial and parental.

4. It is clearly taught that marriage is to be confined to one of each sex. *They twain shall be one flesh.* The same fact is indicated by the equality in number of males and females born into the world. This is found to be the case in all ages and countries.

According to the calculations of those who have made this subject a study, the number of births of males is greater than that of females in the ratio of fourteen to thirteen, thus making allowance for the greater exposure of men to death by hardships on sea and land, and by the perils of war.

5. This union is for life; the two are one flesh, and man is forbidden to put asunder those whom God has thus united.

By the law of the New Testament there is one and but one ground of divorce or separation between husband and wife, and that is a violation, on the part of either, of the seventh commandment.

That commandment refers not only to those who are married, but to all others, enjoining the duty of chastity and purity in thoughts and words as well as in action. On no one subject is the injunction of the wise man to *keep thy heart with all diligence* (Prov. iv, 23) so imperative and so important. Out of the *heart* proceed impure words and actions; and of no vice may it be said with greater truth than of this, that *when lust hath conceived it bringeth forth sin, and sin, when it is finished, bringeth forth death.* James i, 15.

The avoidance of everything that has a tendency to excite impure thoughts is hence an obvious duty. There are many books that seem to have been written for the very purpose of thus leading the young astray. Beautiful pictures are sometimes productive of the same results, and pieces of statuary, representing the human form in various attitudes, may in some instances have a similar tendency.

But worse than all, and more to be dreaded and avoided, is the company of the impure and the lascivious. In no instance is the truth of the declaration of the wise man, that *one sinner destroyeth much good*, (Ecc.

ix, 18,) more clearly seen. It is not easy to escape the contagion of evil example in this respect, and hardly possible to associate with the unclean in conversation or the licentious in conduct without imbibing their sentiments and following their example.

Questions on Lesson XL.

1. What is here said to be a divine institution?
2. What has the civil law to do with marriage?
3. To what must the laws of the land be subordinate?
4. For what are human enactments powerless?
5. How does Jesus Christ prove the institution of marriage to be divine?
6. What is his statement in Matt. xix, 4–6?
7. What is the first inference from this language?
8. What is the second?
9. The third?
10. By what argument is the third inference sustained?
11. What is taught in the fourth place?
12. What fact sustains that position?
13. What proportion do the births of males bear to those of females?
14. What is the fifth point referred to?
15. What is the only scriptural ground of divorce?
16. What is enjoined by the seventh commandment?
17. What is the quotation from the book of Proverbs?
18. What proceed from the heart?

19. What is said by Saint James? (i, 15.)
20. What then is an obvious duty?
21. What are mentioned as calculated to lead the young astray?
22. What is more to be dreaded than bad books and pictures?
23. What is the quotation from Ecclesiastes?

LESSON FORTY-FIRST.

UNTRUTHS, FALSEHOODS, LIES.

A LIE is a false representation designed to deceive. This is a brief but comprehensive definition. We may gather from it several particulars, as for example:

1. The essence of a lie is in the intention. Hence parables, fables, and stories, although the events as related never actually occurred, are not to be included under this designation. The design of the authors was to instruct or amuse, and not to deceive.

2. Not everything that is false or untrue is to be regarded as a lie. An untruth may be told in ignorance, and if that ignorance resulted from a want of sufficient inquiry on

the part of the narrator, we may use the harsher word, falsehood; but unless he designed to deceive, it would be improper to say he told a lie. When Edgar assured his teacher that he knew his lesson he told an untruth, as was very evident when he came to recite; but Edgar really thought he knew it. When he said, "I studied that lesson two hours," he was guilty of a falsehood; for the time, though it seemed longer to Edgar, was only about an hour and a half. He could not have been quite sure that he knew his lesson, perhaps, until he came to the trial; but if he had looked at the clock he would have known that the time spent in study was not two hours. In both instances we suppose it was not his intention to deceive; but in the former, as the result showed, he told an untruth; in the latter a falsehood. It would have been a lie if when he made that statement to the teacher he knew he had not looked at the lesson at all.

3. The guilt of lying may be incurred without the use of language. A false representation designed to deceive may be made by a look or a gesture, or even by silence. Jacob, as related in the twenty-sev-

enth chapter of Genesis, deceived his blind father more by the hairy skin of the kids, with which his hands and neck were covered, than he did by the utterances of his lips. See the account in that chapter from the fifteenth to the twenty-third verse. The pointing of a finger in the wrong direction may mislead a traveler as really as if language were used; and to make no reply to a question when by that silence the questioner is deceived, incurs the same guilt as if a lie were actually uttered.

4. That some person be actually deceived is not an essential ingredient of a lie. It is in the design on the part of him who makes a false representation, and not in the success of the attempted deceit, that the guilt is found. If Jacob's father had at once detected the attempted imposition of his son and denounced it, Jacob's guilt had been none the less. So when Gehazi said, in answer to Elisha's question, "Thy servant went no whither," nobody was deceived; yet for that attempted deception was the liar punished by the infliction of a loathsome disease. Read the account in 2 Kings v, 15–27.

5. It is an error to suppose that the guilt of a lie is any the less when told to one person

than to another. It may be admitted that all persons have not an equal right to demand the truth from us; but it does not follow that we have a right to make a false representation with the design to deceive anybody. Sometimes a little child will ask a question to which it may be thought improper or indelicate to give a truthful answer. In such a case the proper course is plain. We may decline to give any answer at all, on the ground that the question is improper; but there is no warrant for deceiving or for attempting to deceive even an infant.

6. Nor may we make the benefit of the individual whom we attempt to deceive a justification for that attempt. To induce a sick child to take nauseous medicine is sometimes a difficult task. By the utterance of an untruth the child may be deceived and a beneficial result may follow; but that result does not justify the course pursued, nor palliate the guilt incurred by the utterance of a lie.

7. Much less can any supposed benefit that may accrue to ourselves justify the utterance of a willful falsehood. In general terms this proposition will be readily as-

sented to; but in its application it is urged by some ethical writers that there may be exceptions. If a robber meets me on the highway and demands my money, may I tell him a lie and say I have none? Or, if one breaks into the house and asks me where the valuables are, may I give him false information? The answer to these questions must be in the negative. Otherwise we fall into the absurdity that we may do evil that good may come.

8. Finally, a willful lie will lose none of its essential elements even though its utterance were the means of saving life. There are many supposable cases in which adherence to truth may cost life, and in which by a lie it may be saved. The morality of the Bible makes no provision for such cases, and admits of no exception to the command *to put away lying, and to speak every man truth with his neighbor*. Eph. iv, 25.

Questions on Lesson XLI.

1. Give a definition of a lie.
2. What is first inferred from this definition?
3. Why are not parables, fables, and stories included in this designation?
4. What is said in the second place?
5. If an untruth is told in ignorance what may it be called?
6. Can you specify the difference between an untruth, a falsehood, and a lie, as illustrated by Edgar in the text?
7. How may the guilt of lying be incurred in the third place?
8. In what way may false representations be made?
9. How is this illustrated?
10. What may the pointing of a finger do?
11. If no reply is made what may be incurred?
12. What is said not to be essential to a lie?
13. Wherein lies the guilt?
14. Relate the case of Gehazi.
15. What is the fifth remark on the subject?
16. What may be admitted?
17. What does not follow?
18. How is this illustrated?
19. What is said of deceiving for another's benefit?
20. And what of benefiting ourselves?
21. Mention some supposed exceptions?
22. What absurdity is alluded to?
23. Suppose a lie were the means of saving life, would that justify its utterance?
24. What is the quotation from Ephesians iv, 25?

LESSON FORTY-SECOND.

TRUTHFULNESS.

THE sin of deception by the utterance of willful falsehoods has been variously estimated by teachers of morality. Plato, one of the wisest of the ancient heathen philosophers, taught that he may lie who knows how to do it at a suitable time: in other words, that the guilt is found not in the utterance of the falsehood, but in its detection. This is seen at once to be a license for every kind of deception. Every liar persuades himself that his falsehood will not be detected and exposed. Did this doctrine universally prevail, we should not know whom to trust or in whom to confide, and society could scarcely exist.

Professedly Christian writers have taught sentiments equally loose and unscriptural. It is said of the learned Origen that he gave it as his opinion that falsehoods might be told without incurring guilt when their object was to promote the interests of a good cause. The Jesuits acted in accordance with this sentiment when, in preaching to the Indians, they represented Jesus Christ as a great warrior, who had slain multitudes of his enemies, and adorned his wigwam with their scalps. Their object was to convert the red men of the forest to Christianity—a good object, certainly, but one not likely to be attained by such preaching; and even if it were, affording no justification for the promulgation of so monstrous a falsehood. Origen's sentiment, like that of Plato, if reduced to general practice, would in a little while banish from the world mutual trust and confidence between man and his fellows. The liar can easily persuade himself that his attempts to deceive are made with a good object, and he being permitted to be the judge in his own case, may gratify his propensity to any extent.

Dr. Paley teaches that a falsehood is not criminal if told to a person who has no right to know the truth, or if no inconvenience is likely to be occasioned by it. But who is to decide as to the amount of inconvenience that will result in any given case, or to draw the line and say, Inconvenience to this extent makes the falsehood criminal, but anything less would be excusable? And then how easy a thing to persuade one's self that this or that individual has no right to know the truth! It is said that the Romish Church teaches that inasmuch as heretics, by which they mean all who are not of their faith, have no right to know the truth, therefore it is proper to deceive them by the utterance of willful falsehoods. A moment's reflection will show that this sentiment cannot be correct, and that the criminality of a falsehood has nothing to do with the convenience or inconvenience of the person to whom it is told. Equally clear is it that even though there may be those of whom it may be said that they have no right to know the truth, that fact can never justify us in telling a lie even to them. It is said, indeed, that on one occasion General Washington deceived the enemy by a falsehood, and some have argued that he was justifiable in so doing. It is better, and more in accordance with the ethics of the Bible, to admit that on that occasion, if it did occur, the father of his country did wrong; for if the principle be admitted that we may lie to those who have no right to know the truth, it will not be a difficult matter to excuse almost every falsehood.

The teachings of the Bible on this subject are clear and explicit. Our heavenly Father is frequently called the God of truth. Deut. xxxii, 4; Psa. xxxi, 5; Rev. vi, 10. Jesus Christ styles himself *the Truth*, as well as the way and the life. John xiv, 6. On the other hand it is said of man's arch adversary, the devil, that there is no *truth in him; that he is a liar, and the father of it.* John viii, 44. Injunctions to speak the truth are numerous. *He that speaketh truth showeth forth righteousness; and the lip of truth shall be established forever.* Prov. xii, 17, 19. The psalmist in his prayer to the Almighty says: *Thou desirest truth in the inward parts*, (Psa. li, 6;) and in portraying the character of the man who shall dwell in the holy hill (or city) of the Lord, he tells us that, among other things, *he speaketh the truth in his heart.* Both in the Old Testament and in the New the command is, *Speak ye every man the truth to his neighbor.* Zech. viii, 16. Ephes. iv, 25. On the other hand it is written, *Ye shall not lie one to another.* Lev. xix, 11. *The mouth that speaketh lies shall be stopped.* Psa. lxiii, 11. *Lying lips are abomination to the Lord.* Prov. xii, 22. Finally, not to multiply quo-

15

tations, as we might to a great extent, this is the fearful declaration of God's word: *All liars shall have their part in the lake which burneth with fire and brimstone, which is the second death.* Rev. xxi, 8.

Questions on Lesson XLII.

1. How have moralists estimated the sin of falsehood?
2. What was Plato?
3. What did he teach on the subject of lying?
4. What would result from that doctrine?
5. What was the opinion of Origen?
6. What is said of the Jesuits?
7. What was their object?
8. What would be the effect of Origen's doctrine?
9. What does Dr. Paley teach on the subject?
10. Show the fallacy of his teaching in these instances?
11. What does the Romish Church teach relative to heretics?
12. Whom do they mean by heretics?
13. Is their teaching correct?
14. Do you think there are any who have no right to know the truth on any given subject?
15. If there are, what then?
16. What is said of General Washington?
17. What is said of the teachings of the Bible?
18. What is our heavenly Father called?
19. What does Jesus style himself?

20. What do the Scriptures say of the devil?
21. Give some of the passages quoted relative to truth.
22. Some of those having reference to the guilt of lying.

LESSON FORTY-THIRD.

PROMISE BREAKING.

The character of a liar is esteemed disgraceful by all classes of men. To speak the truth to one another seems to be essentially necessary even among thieves and robbers when banded together for the accomplishment of their wicked object. The poet carries the idea so far as to assure us that

> Devil with devil damned firm compact holds.

How utterly vile then must be the character of a boy or girl who has acquired this habit and indulges in it. In society no greater insult can be offered than to call an individual a liar, and yet some do not scruple to *be* what they would regard it the greatest possible insult to be called.

We have seen what are the teachings of the Bible on the subject, and noticed some of those methods by which truth is violated. There are many other methods:

1. *Promise breaking* does not fall exactly within our definition of lying. Generally there is no intention to break a promise when it is given; but afterward something occurs that renders it not so easy to perform, or not so pleasant, and the promise is broken and the guilt of a lie is incurred. The guilt is not quite so great as it would have been if the promise had been made with the intention of violating it; but the injury to the disappointed party is the same; and he who wishes to keep a conscience void of offense will aim to be very exact in the fulfillment of every promise.

In the psalmist's description of a good man, he says of him that *he sweareth to his own hurt and changeth not*, (Psa. xv, 4;) that is, that no possible inconvenience to himself will prevent him from fulfilling a promise solemnly given. Such, evidently, should be the universal rule.

The person to whom a promise is made has a right to release from the obligation of fulfilling it; but otherwise there are only two ways in which they who have made promises may be excusable for not performing them. The one is where circumstances that have since arisen are such as to render the performance impossible; and the other, where the promise cannot be fulfilled without committing sin. If you should fall and break your leg you would be excusable for not keeping your engagement to run a foot race this afternoon; and Samuel's reason for not meeting a party of schoolmates who were going to the woods for nuts was quite sufficient. His father had refused permission for him to go, and Samuel could not have kept his promise to the boys without disobeying his father, which he had no right to do. In such cases there is really a condition implied, if not expressed, upon which the promise depends; and it would be well in all cases if the condition were expressed at the time the promise is given. Such is the teaching of the apostle. *Whereas ye know not what shall be on the morrow, ye ought to say, If the Lord will we shall live and do this or that.* James iv, 14, 15.

In a former lesson we alluded to the loose morality prevalent among the ancients on this subject. We close this chapter with an illustrious instance of devotion to truth evinced by a heathen idolater, to whom life beyond the grave was an unsolved problem. It is an instance of promise-keeping which may cause the blush of shame upon the cheek of many who bear the Christian name. The Roman general, Regulus, was taken prisoner by the Carthaginians. After keeping him in confinement for several years they sent him back to Rome to propose an exchange of prisoners, having first taken from him an oath that he would return to his prison if his proposition were not accepted. The Romans rejected the proposal; and, to the surprise of all, Regulus prepared to return to his enemies. He had promised to return, and he held his promise sacred; nor could he be moved from it by the entreaties of his friends, or the tears of his wife and children. He knew, too, that death by torture awaited him if he ventured again into the hands of the Carthaginians; but he had promised to return. He did return, and was put to death by the most cruel torments that his enemies could devise. "His enemies," says the historian, (Rollin,) "by depriving him of some days, perhaps years of life, brought eternal infamy on themselves."

Questions on Lesson XLIII.

1. What is said of a liar?
2. What seems essential among thieves?
3. What sentiment is quoted from the poet?
4. Do you think the sentiment is correct?
5. What is said must be utterly vile?
6. What is the greatest insult one man can offer to another?
7. What is the subject of this lesson?
8. In what sense does promise-breaking usually differ from lying?
9. What is said of the guilt incurred by it?
10. What of the injury to the disappointed?
11. What of him who wishes to keep a conscience void of offense?
12. Give the psalmist's description of a good man.
13. Explain it.
14. Who can release from the performance of a promise?
15. How many other ways are there of being released?
16. What are they?
17. Illustrate the first.
18. The second.
19. When these promises were made what was implied?
20. What says St. James on conditional promises?
21. Can you relate the story of Regulus?

LESSON FORTY-FOURTH.

PREVARICATION, EQUIVOCATION, EXAGGERATION.

Among the methods by which the guilt of lying is incurred we notice

2. *The practice of keeping back a part when we profess to tell the whole truth.* This is one very common mode of what is called prevarication. What is said may be strictly correct, but if something more be necessary to the integrity of a narration the hearer may be as really deceived as if the story had been false from beginning to end.

It is related of Abraham, afterward known as the father of the faithful, that for fear of the Egyptians he said of his wife Sarah, "She is my sister." Gen. xii, 19. In a certain sense that was true. She was his step-sister, but she was also his wife, and it was that fact which he meant to deny or conceal. The sacred writer relates the case without comment for our admonition; leaving a blot upon the character of Abraham, and showing us how he fell into the very danger which he hoped, by prevarication, to avoid, and how he was rebuked for his conduct by the idolatrous heathen.

In the New Testament we have a more striking illustration of this vice and of the guilt incurred by indulgence in it. A man, by name Ananias, and his wife Sapphira, owned a piece of property which they sold, and brought a portion of the money to the apostles to put into a common fund for the benefit of the Church at large. This was very well, and was perhaps as much as could have been expected from them. But they tried to impose upon their brethren. They both said, "We sold the land for so much," that is, for the sum which they brought to the treasury. They did sell the land for so much, and for something more. It was the keeping back of this latter part of the statement that was intended to deceive, and that the apostles call lying, lying not to men merely, but to God. It was for this, a crime which some even at this day are disposed to regard as trivial, that such sudden and terrible punishment was inflicted by the God of truth, the God with whom we have to do. Acts v, 1–10.

3. Near akin to this mode of deception is the use of words and phrases of ambig-

uous or doubtful meaning, resulting in what is usually styled *equivocation*. When a traveler, crossing a stream on horseback, was told, in answer to his question to a boy who stood upon the bank that the bottom was hard, he rode in boldly. When his horse floundered in the mud it was no relief to be told that he had not yet reached the bottom, nor did the wit of the youngster in any sense lesson the guilt of the lie by which the traveler had been deceived.

The boy who, when he was asked why he was late at school, told the teacher that he had been sent on an errand by his mother, did not state what was in itself false; but nevertheless was guilty of a lie by equivocation. He had been sent on an errand, but was back in ample time to be at school in good season. The true answer would have been, "I am late, because I loitered by the way."

4. A still more common practice is that of *exaggeration*. This is, by many, so frequently indulged that they seem scarcely to be aware of what they are saying. Their conversation abounds in adjectives of the superlative degree, and that was the name by which a little girl of my acquaintance

was sometimes designated by her teacher at a large boarding-school. She was called Miss Superlative, because of her unhappy propensity to exaggerate almost every subject about which she had anything to say. Happily in her case the use of that nickname had the desired effect, and she broke herself of the bad habit.

It was not so in the case of a young minister as told by Bishop Hedding. At one of the conferences where the good man presided a preacher was charged with indulging to great excess in the use of exaggeration. He was not said to be guilty of falsehood; but superlatives flowed so freely from his tongue that truth had all the semblance and frequently did all the mischief of a lie. The young man was sentenced to be publicly admonished by the chair. The bishop with great kindness pointed out the evils resulting from the habit, when the accused acknowledged his faults and uttered a solemn vow of amendment. "I regret the habit," said he; "I have struggled against it, and wept over it. Yes," he continued, "I can truly say it has already caused me to shed barrels of tears."

Questions on Lesson XLIV.

1. What is the next method of violating truth?
2. What is it usually called?
3. What did Abraham say of Sarah?
4. In what sense was that true?
5. What fact did he want to conceal?
6. For what purpose does Moses relate this case?
7. What resulted from Abraham's prevarication?
8. What illustration have we in the New Testament?
9. Give an outline of the case of Ananias and his wife.
10. What did the apostle call their prevarication?
11. What mode of deception is next mentioned?
12. What is said of the traveler?
13. What of the boy who was late at school?
14. In what consisted his guilt?
15. What is said of exaggeration?
16. What does the conversation of some persons abound in?
17. What was the little girl called?
18. Why?
19. What effect was produced by the nickname?
20. What story is told to show the inveteracy of this bad habit?

LESSON FORTY-FIFTH.

FLATTERY, TALE-BEARING, SLANDER, PERJURY.

5. A FLATTERER is one who seeks to excite another's self-love by adulation. He is not necessarily, but almost always a liar, and is generally actuated by selfish motives. Did he not hope to gain something by it, he would hardly go out of his way to utter flatteries; and when he is bent upon his object, a falsehood will generally better serve his purpose than the truth. So long ago as the time of Solomon it was said that *a flattering mouth worketh ruin,* (Prov. xxvi, 28;) and the advice of the wise man is as appropriate now as when it was first uttered: *Meddle not with him that flattereth with his lips.* Prov. xx, 19. A species of flattery is sometimes practiced by written recommendations of individuals or of their wares. A man writes a book, or invents a machine, or becomes an agent for a public institution, and seeks a favorable notice from one better known to the public than himself. It requires some decision to refuse so small a

favor; but it evinces a lax morality to give an attestation beyond what is known to be the strict truth.

6. *Tale-bearing* is another vice which almost always includes the utterance of what is exaggerated or false. Indeed, it is hardly possible to repeat a story to the injury of another's character without distorting and coloring the facts in the case, and thus incurring the guilt of lying. The Scriptures abound in denunciations of the practice. *Thou shalt not go up and down as a tale-bearer among thy people.* Lev. xix, 16. *The words of a tale-bearer are as wounds.* Prov. xxvi, 20. The Apostle Peter classes the *busy-body in other men's matters* with the murderer and the thief. 1 Peter iv, 15. It is sometimes necessary to expose the evil doings of another. When such is the case, and the duty is plain, no fear of being called a tell-tale ought to deter from it. But this is a very different thing from tale-bearing, which always implies a readiness to injure another in his feelings or his reputation, and is one of the meanest vices.

7. *Slander* is a malicious story uttered for the purpose of injuring another. It is several degrees worse than ordinary tale-bear-

ing, which is sometimes indulged in from mere want of thought, without the malicious purpose which characterizes slander. It has been well said that it takes two to make a slander, one to utter it and another to listen to it. No one would be at the trouble to invent a slander if he could find none to hearken to his story, and there is no surer way to put a stop to its circulation than to turn a deaf ear to the inventor. On the contrary, those who listen complacently to injurious reports about others do, in fact, participate in the guilt of the slanderer; and he who repeats a falsehood is quite as blameworthy as he who invented it, and may, indeed, be the means of doing a far greater amount of injury. A person of very little reputation may start a story to the injury of another, and few will give credit to the report; but suppose you, having heard it, do not stop to inquire into its truth, but repeat it; you thus give it currency where otherwise it had never been heard of, and others repeat as coming from you what, coming from another, they would have deemed unworthy of notice. Thus it will be seen that the guilt of slander may be incurred without the utterance of falsehood.

It is merely necessary to repeat what you have heard, and though you do not vouch for its truth, you commit as grievous a wrong as if you had invented the story. And who shall estimate the greatness of the injury inflicted by the tongue of slander? Reputation ought to be dearer than the wealth of the world. So the Bible teaches us: *A good name is better than great riches.* Prov. xxii, 1. But the slanderer seeks to destroy a good name, and, with feelings that we can imagine as only finding their counterpart in the regions of the lost, he endeavors to rob its possessor of that which is to him beyond all price, but which can be of no use or value to the spoiler.

8. The last and most grievous violation of truth is known as *Perjury*, which is the utterance of a willful lie, and the calling upon God to bear witness to it. Of all sins of the tongue this is the most atrocious. By the laws of the land it is punishable with imprisonment, and one of the most startling evidences of human depravity is found in the fact that in this Christian land, at almost every court of criminal jurisprudence, some are indicted for this crime, found guilty, and imprisoned. The temptation to

perjury is usually a little gain, or a temporary advantage over an opponent. Of course such a temptation is only yielded to by those who have previously indulged themselves in the habit of lying, and the only security any of us can have against being led into the same snare, and falling into the same dreadful condemnation, is a steadfast determination, by God's grace, to adhere under all circumstances strictly to the truth.

Questions on Lesson XLV.

1. How do you define a *flatterer?*
2. Is a flatterer always a liar?
3. By what class of motives is he usually actuated?
4. What does Solomon say of a flattering mouth?
5. Do you remember Solomon's advice on the subject?
6. What is usually included in *tale-bearing?*
7. Can you repeat what is said in Lev. xix, 16?
8. To what does Solomon compare the words of a tale-bearer?
9. With whom does Paul class the tale-bearer?
10. What is said with regard to being called a tell-tale?
11. Give a definition of *slander.*
12. Wherein does it differ from ordinary tale-bearing?
13. What has been well said?
14. How may the circulation of a slander be stopped?

15. What is said of listening to slanderous reports?
16. What of him who repeats them?
17. Can one who adheres to truth be guilty of slander?
18. What does the Bible teach about reputation?
19. What does the slanderer seek to destroy?
20. Define *perjury*.
21. What is the character of this sin?
22. How is it punished by the laws of the land?
23. What startling evidence of depravity is here noticed?
24. What is the usual temptation to perjury?
25. Who yield to such temptations?
26. What is our security?

LESSON FORTY-SIXTH.

PROFANENESS.

THE commandment which forbids the taking of God's name in vain is one of the most solemn in the decalogue. It is the only one to which a positive threatening is annexed. It assures us that the Lord will not hold him guiltless that taketh his name in vain; that is, God will most assuredly take notice of every violation of this law and punish the transgressor.

God's name is taken in vain,

1. *When it is used lightly and irreverently.* In ordinary conversation, without thought, that name is frequently used, and with some its use has become so habitual that they are scarcely aware of the frequency with which they thus transgress. We regard the Jews who would not utter Jehovah's name aloud even when reading the sacred Scriptures as foolishly superstitious. In that superstition there was at least nothing sinful, which cannot be said of a practice which sometimes prevails in the pulpit, and which induced a little unsophisticated child to suppose that a certain minister was swearing in that sacred place. HIS name is to be used only with reverence, and the introduction to the prayer taught us by the Saviour should ever be present in our thoughts when those thoughts are turned toward our Father in heaven: *Hallowed be thy name.*

That name is taken in vain,

2. *By perjury or false swearing.* On this monstrous wickedness we made some remarks in the preceding lesson. It is unnecessary to repeat them, nor need we add more upon the subject than to say it is not possible to conceive how His name can be more flagrantly and insolently taken in vain

than by solemnly calling upon him to bear witness to what is known to be a lie.

His name is taken in vain,

3. *By all unnecessary oaths.* Were it not for the depravity of the human heart, and for the fact that *the wicked go astray as soon as they be born, speaking lies*, (Psa. lviii, 3,) an oath would never be necessary. As it is, nothing but the requirements of the law of the land, as in the case of a witness or a juror, will justify an appeal to the Most High for the truth of testimony or the conscientiousness of a verdict. It is indeed a disputed point whether, even in such cases, it is not better solemnly to affirm, without making an appeal to the Supreme Being; and most courts of justice recognize such conscientious scruples and accept an affirmation in place of an oath. This being the case, at least in our own country, there seems to be no absolute necessity for invoking God's name at all; and it is most certain that he who does not invoke it will not be likely to take it in vain. On this subject the apostle James is very explicit: *Above all things, my brethren, swear not, neither by heaven, neither by the earth, neither by any other oath; but let your yea be yea, and your*

nay, nay. James v, 12. There are those who understand this language literally, and make no exceptions even for judicial oaths. If such were the sentiment of the entire community, and the practice of kissing the Bible or appealing to God by lifting the right hand were utterly abolished in favor of solemn affirmation, the ends of justice would be as well served, and the temptation to violate the third commandment greatly lessened.

4. The Saviour taught very clearly that all swearing, whether the name of the Supreme Being be invoked or not, is a transgression of the third commandment. In his day it seems that it was quite common, even in conversation, to swear by heaven, by the earth, by Jerusalem, and by the temple. These oaths were not considered binding; and even those who held to the sanctity of what they deemed an oath did not regard such swearing as criminal. They were like those of our own day who, although they would by no means take a false oath, do not hesitate to intersperse their conversation with such phrases as By Jupiter, By George, By Jingo, By heaven, and the like. Christ teaches that all this is swearing, and is forbidden. *Whoso shall swear by the temple*

sweareth by it and by him that dwelleth therein; and he that shall swear by heaven sweareth by the throne of God and by him that sitteth thereon. Matt. xxiii, 21, 22. In his sermon on the mount the great Teacher expressly says, *Swear not at all: but let your communication be yea, yea, nay, nay; for whatsoever is more than these cometh of evil.* Matt. v, 34–37. That is, anything more than a mere affirmation or denial in ordinary conversation is wrong.

Questions on Lesson XLVI.

1. What is the subject of this lesson?
2. By which of the commandments is swearing forbidden?
3. What is peculiar to this commandment?
4. What is the meaning of the threatening annexed to it?
5. How is his name taken in vain?
6. What is said of the conscientious Jews?
7. What is said of that superstition?
8. What is the preface to the Lord's Prayer?
9. What is another method of transgressing this commandment?
10. What is the third?
11. Why are oaths ever necessary?
12. What may be done in courts of justice by those who have scruples about taking an oath?

13. Will affirmation answer the same purpose?
14. What says St. James on the subject?
15. May the apostle be understood literally in this matter?
16. What did the Saviour teach about swearing?
17. What was common in his day?
18. Were such oaths deemed binding?
19. What did they resemble in our day?
20. Can you repeat the Saviour's language on the subject?

LESSON FORTY-SEVENTH.

SWEARING.

By the prophet Hosea, (iv, 2,) *swearing* is classed with *lying*, and *killing*, and *stealing*, and *committing adultery;* and Jeremiah says, (xxiii, 10,) *Because of swearing the land mourneth.* A few things may be said concerning this vice, which, while they set forth some of its peculiarities, may serve as warnings against it, and as dissuasives from it.

And first, it is a vice to which the temptation must be very small. In almost every other act of transgression, some profit or pleasure is held out as the result to be attained. Comparing transgressors to the different kinds of fish which are allured by the skillfully prepared bait, the swearer is justly regarded as the most silly of them all. He bites at the naked hook. He who has made most proficiency in the art, and who practices it with the greatest assiduity, will find it difficult to say what of profit or pleasure he has derived from it.

Then, again, what little gratification there is in swearing arises entirely from the fact that it is sinning against God. Why does the swearer take HIS name in vain? Why do we hear that name in the bold blasphemy of youth, in the faltering profanity of childhood, in the driveling curses of old age? It is hard to find any other reason than the simple fact that HE has forbidden it, and that the swearer knows he has forbidden it. Nay, we can scarcely conceive that man's ingenuity would have found any gratification in taking God's name in vain had not the commandment absolutely forbidden it.

A gentleman in the company of some profane swearers, who had been indulging in the habit quite profusely, told them a story to which they listened attentively. It was a tale of interest, but the relator interlarded it continually with the expression, "Shovel, Poker, and Tongs." Almost every sentence ended with the words shovel, poker, and tongs, or poker, shovel, and tongs, or shovel, tongs, and poker. When he finished, his hearers asked the reason of his frequent iteration of these words; to which he replied, "That's my way of swearing," which they were constrained to admit was quite as sensible, if not as wicked, as their own.

Almost every other sin seeks concealment; the swearer has no gratification unless there are some present to hear him. We cannot, indeed, speak with positive certainty on the subject, but it is believed that there is very little profane swearing done in secret. Every oath seems to be a challenge not only to those around to listen, but to HIM whose name is blasphemed to hearken and punish.

Has the profane swearer any other object than to show his hardihood by insulting his Maker to his face? Possibly he may have one other. It is by his example to lead his companions and associates into the same guilt. And it is wonderful with what ease this is done. A swearer cannot be long in any company without inducing some to fall into the same habit. He is like one infected with a contagious disease. The only safety is in shunning his company, and everybody ought to shun it until he abandons a habit so vile and so God-dishonoring.

But it is a habit that is not easily abandoned. There is scarcely any vice that takes hold so deeply, or becomes so permanently incorporated with the moral character. At first the young imitator trembles as he takes his Maker's name in vain, and shudders at the sound of his own blaspheming. By continuing the practice the habit grows upon him. Soon he can swear as glibly as his teachers. He is now a teacher of others. An oath, a curse, a blasphemous expression becomes to him as natural as to open his lips. For a while, indeed, he is careful as to the company in which he ventures to give utterance to profane language. He does not swear in presence of his mother or his sisters; but the restraint is irksome, and is soon thrown off. He swears at all times and in all places, and the fearful probability is that he will take with him into the eternal world the character of a profane swearer, and meet his doom at the bar of that awful

Being whom he has been in the constant habit of insulting to his face, and who has declared that he will not hold him guiltless who taketh his name in vain.

The only safety with reference to this vice is in steadfastly resisting its earliest indications. No one ever became a profane swearer at once. Boys are led into the habit by the use of phrases which have in them no meaning. By Gemini, By Jingo, By Golly, and similar phrases prepare the way for bolder efforts, and those who indulge in them are led on step by step, almost imperceptibly, until they take their places in the ranks of the profane.

Questions on Lesson XLVII.

1. What sins are classed with swearing by the prophet Hosea?
2. Repeat Jeremiah xxiii, 10.
3. What is said of the temptation to swear?
4. What is held out in every other act of transgression?
5. What is said of the swearer as compared with other transgressors?
6. Whence arises the gratification of swearing?
7. Is it likely men would swear if God had not forbidden it?

8. What is said of a gentleman in the company of swearers?
9 What peculiarity of swearing is here mentioned?
10. Do men swear much in secret?
11. To whom does an oath seem to be a challenge?
12. How does the profane swearer show his hardihood?
13. What other motive may he have?
14. Do swearers easily make proselytes?
15. What is a swearer said to be like?
16. What is the only safe course?
17. Is the habit, when once acquired, easily abandoned?
18. What is said of the vice?
19. How is the career of the swearer traced out?
20. What is the result?
21. How will he, in all probability, go into the eternal world?
22. What is the only safety?

LESSON FORTY-EIGHTH.

THE SABBATH—ITS INSTITUTION AND DESIGN.

THE institution of a weekly day of rest dates from the creation. Moses tells us that *God rested on the seventh day from all his work which he had made.* Gen. ii, 2.

On this occasion he tells us also that *God blessed the seventh day and sanctified it, because that in it he had rested from all his work.* Gen. ii, 3. It could not have been on his own account that the Lord rested, as if the work of creation had wearied him. Nor was it for his own sake that he blessed that day, for with him it is evident that all days must be alike; if, indeed, in eternity there be any such thing as the succession of time. This information, then, is given on our account; and for us the day of rest was designed, as saith the Saviour, *The Sabbath was made for man.* Mark ii, 27.

The phraseology of the. fourth commandment, *Remember the Sabbath day to keep it holy*, (Ex. xx, 8,) seems to imply that it was not then given for the first time and that indeed it was a command from the beginning. That it has a place among the laws given from Mount Sinai is proof that it was designed to be perpetual and to be binding upon all people. Those who take a different view of the subject ought to be able to tell us why this commandment has a place in the moral law, if it were not intended to be of equal force and authority with the others, which were written at the same time on two tables of stone by the finger of God.

The design of the Sabbath is clearly taught in the Bible. It was intended, in the first place, *to commemorate that great work of the Almighty, the creation of the universe.* It is common to set apart certain days which are kept in honor of events that are deemed of sufficient importance. Thus the twenty-fifth of December is observed by Christians as the anniversary of our Saviour's birth; and the fourth of July is kept in the United States as a memorial of the signing of the Declaration of Independence.

It seems fitting that a work of such infinitely transcending importance should be commemorated with greater frequency; and once a week is not too often to devote to a contemplation of the wonderful goodness, wisdom, and power of God as evinced by the creation.

In the second place the Sabbath is intended *as a day of rest.* As we have seen, labor of some kind is essential to man's well-being. Intervals of rest are equally essential. He who formed us and gave us the capacity for toil has also provided seasons of rest, and has found it necessary to command cessation from all labor one day in every seven. In this command he has included all beasts of burden. They also need a weekly day of rest; and it has been found by experience that the horse, for instance, will actually live longer, do more work, and be of more profit to his owner, if permitted to enjoy what his Maker intended for him a day's rest in every seven. Thus the wisdom as well as the goodness of God is seen in this provision.

The Sabbath was also intended *as a special season of religious worship*, and the wisdom of God is shown in the setting apart of a specific day for that purpose. It is true God may be worshiped acceptably at any time; but it is equally true that the recurrence of a day for that object tends to keep alive the importance of the duty; and it is a fact that where the Sabbath is unobserved there the worship of the Most High is unknown or neglected.

Again: the day is designed *not only for religious worship, but for moral improvement*, for the study of divine truth, and for progressive advancement in Christian knowledge. The mind, being exempted from the cares and anxieties of business and of worldly pursuits, has one day in every seven which it may devote especially to the acquisition of that wisdom which cometh down from the Father of lights, while everything around, the quiet stillness, the assemblages for worship, prayer, and praise, all unite to make such studies attractive and profitable.

Finally, the Sabbath is regarded in the Scriptures *as a type of that endless rest* which remains for the people of God in another world. *There remaineth*, says the apostle, *a rest;* or, as it is in the margin, *a keeping of Sabbath for the people of God.* Heb. iv, 9. In the midst of all the turmoil of life, its cares, and anxieties, and troubles, there recurs every week a day of calm repose, a universal memento of our resting place in heaven, while the duties of each recurring Sabbath are mercifully designed to fit us for its purity and endless peace.

QUESTIONS ON LESSON XLVIII.

1. When was the Sabbath instituted?
2. What did God do on the seventh day?
3. Why did he bless and sanctify the Sabbath day?
4. Do you suppose that the Lord rested on his own account?
5. What must all days be with him?
6. For whom was the Sabbath instituted?
7. What saith the Saviour on the subject?
8. Can you repeat the fourth commandment?
9. What seems to be implied by the first word in this commandment?
10. What is inferred from the fact that it was given from Mount Sinai?
11. Where is taught the design of the Sabbath?
12. What was it intended to commemorate?
13. What is commemorated on the 25th of December?
14. Of what is the 4th of July the memorial?
15. For what other purpose was the Sabbath intended?
16. What are said to be equally essential with labor?
17. What are included in this command besides human beings?
18. What is said of the horse?
19. What is said of the Sabbath as a special season of religious worship?
20. What is the fact in those places where the Sabbath is not observed?
21. Mention other purposes for which the day is appropriate.
22. How are religious studies rendered attractive on the Sabbath?

23. Of what do the Scriptures teach us to regard the Sabbath as a type?
24. What recurs every week?
25. For what are the duties of the Sabbath designed to fit us?

LESSON FORTY-NINTH.

THE SABBATH: CHANGE OF THE DAY: MANNER OF OBSERVANCE.

After the resurrection of Jesus Christ, and in commemoration of that most wonderful event, the day of rest, or Sabbath, was changed from the seventh day of the week, or Saturday, to the first, or Sunday. This was done by the apostles, under the inspiration of the Holy Ghost, with the sanction of the Saviour.

By all who receive the New Testament, with a very few exceptions, the first day of the week is recognized as the Sabbath, or the Lord's day, as it was by the early Christians.

From the Acts of the Apostles (xx, 7) we learn that it was on the first day of the week that the disciples assembled to break bread, (that is, to celebrate the Lord's Supper,) and that on that day the Apostle Paul preached unto them the Gospel. From 1 Cor. xvi, 1, 2, we learn that it was on the first day of the week that Christians held their meetings for religious worship; and the Apostle John says, *I was in the Spirit on the Lord's day.* Rev. i, 10. And thence onward to the present time the testimony of history is uniform as to the observance of the first day of the week as the Sabbath. True, there are those who prefer to call the first day of the week the Lord's day, to which there can be no objection, provided it is understood and acknowledged that all the sanctities pertain to it which are enjoined with reference to the Sabbath.

The design and the objects for which the day was set apart remain the same as they were previous to its change, with the addition that now the day, as it recurs every week, is intended not only to commemorate the goodness, wisdom, and power of God as seen in creation, but also to bring vividly before the mind the resurrection of our Lord from the dead, an event, without exception, the greatest and most important that ever took place in our world.

As to the manner of its observance, it

may be said, in general terms, that we are required totally to abstain on the Lord's day from everything that may not be comprehended in one or other of the three general divisions: 1. Works of necessity; 2. Deeds of mercy; 3. Acts tending to religious improvement.

1. *Works of necessity* cannot be specifically enumerated. What may at one time come under this head may not be necessary at another; and a work that may, with propriety, be performed by one individual, may not have the same justification when done by another. In the early history of this country it is related that frequently, when the people assembled for divine worship, some were obliged to stand guard with loaded muskets, to prevent attacks from hostile Indians. At the time that may have been a work of necessity, and therefore justifiable. We have reason to be thankful that there is no necessity for anything of the kind now.

So too it may be necessary for a minister, who has to preach to two or three congregations, to saddle his horse and ride several miles on the Lord's day. But this fact will not excuse others for doing the same.

In this, as in many other things pertaining to Christian morals, a great deal is left to the conscience of each individual. Before engaging in any work on the Sabbath ask yourself: Is this a work of necessity, and is it necessary that I should do it to-day? If both questions cannot be readily answered in the affirmative it will be safe to let it alone.

One Sunday morning it was found that Thomas had forgotten to clean his shoes on Saturday night. The question arose, Shall he do it now? and that question involved another, Is it *necessary* that his shoes should be cleaned? It was hardly possible to say yes to that question. It might be pleasant and agreeable, but it could hardly be called necessary. So, on the whole, it is better for him to wear them to church as they are. The little mortification that he may feel will perhaps cause him to be more mindful of his Saturday night's duty hereafter. Possibly, too, if he allows himself to regard wearing clean shoes on Sunday as necessary, he will gradually come to regard other things, in favor of which even less can be said, as also necessary.

Questions on Lesson XLIX.

1. What was changed after Christ's resurrection?
2. Why was it changed to the first day of the week?
3. By whom was this change made?
4. Had they authority to make the change?
5. Is the first day of the week generally regarded as the Sabbath?
6. What do we learn from Acts xx, 7?
7. What do you understand by breaking bread in the New Testament?
8. From what passage of Scripture do we infer that the early Christians met for worship on the first day of the week?
9. What does John say in Rev. i, 10?
10. What is the testimony of history on the subject?
11. What do some prefer to call the first day of the week?
12. Is there any objection to its being called the Lord's day?
13. Are the design and objects of the Sabbath the same as they were before the day was changed?
14. What great fact is now commemorated by the Sabbath?
15. What is here said of Christ's resurrection?
16. What three classes of duty may be performed on the Sabbath?
17. What is said of works of necessity?
18. What happened in the early history of this country?
19. What must be left to conscience?
20. What two questions are suggested?

21. What had Thomas forgotten?
22. What question then arose?
23. What other question was involved?
24. How was it answered?
25. What will probably result from his mortification?
26. What would follow if he took the other course?

LESSON FIFTIETH.

THE SABBATH; WORKS OF MERCY; RELIGIOUS IMPROVEMENT.

God says by the prophet Hosea, (vi, 6,) *I desired mercy and not sacrifice;* that is, I prefer deeds of benevolence and kindness to acts of mere external obedience. Jesus Christ refers to the same passage when he rebukes the Jews for their superstitious adherence to the mere letter of the law. They charged him with breaking the Sabbath because he healed the sick on that day. (Matt. xii, 10, Luke xiii, 14.) Both by example and by precept he taught us that it is right to perform deeds of mercy on the Sabbath, and that these deeds of mercy refer not only to the bodies and souls of our fellow-creatures, but also to dumb beasts. It is an act of mercy to supply horses and other cattle with food and drink on the Sabbath, and *if one of them be fallen into a pit, straightway to pull him out*, (Luke xiv, 5;) or by the same reasoning, if a dumb creature meets with any other accident, or is taken sick, to render all the assistance in our power. *It is lawful to do well on the Sabbath days.* Matt. xii, 12.

A word of caution may here be necessary, and that is, to be most careful that we do not deceive ourselves with reference to acts of mercy. We may make them a mere pretense for neglecting the appropriate duties of the Sabbath, as, for instance, by taking a long walk for our own enjoyment, and calling at the house of a sick friend, and there sitting down to rest until it is time to return home. Possibly we may impose on the invalid as having "done well" by calling to see him instead of going to church; but it is not likely that He who commands us to keep his day holy will be deceived by our conduct, or mistake the motives by which we are actuated.

A second caution may be added. From the fact that the Sabbath is called the day of rest some seem disposed to spend its hours in idleness. They cut off a piece from each end of the day by rising in the morning a little later, and by retiring to bed a little earlier than on other days. This is a manifest perversion of the Sabbath. Idleness is as displeasing in His sight on Sunday as at any other time. The Sabbath is indeed to be a day of rest, and in this respect a type of heaven; but the rest is from the cares and anxieties of the world, and not from the service of God; and though it is said of those who have gone thither that they rest from their *labors*, yet are we taught that they are unceasingly engaged in studying and doing *his* will. Imagination cannot picture such a thing as a lazy angel in heaven.

The third class of duties appropriate to the Sabbath are such as tend to the religious improvement of ourselves and others. No one has reached a point beyond which he may not increase in the acquisition of divine knowledge, and scarcely any one knows so little as not to find some to whom he may impart instruction. For purposes of this kind of improvement we are abundantly furnished with the necessary means. The Bible is within the reach of all, and there are very few who have not access to books written to make plainer its instructions.

In the family circle and in the Sunday-school, as well as in the public congregation which statedly assembles for divine worship, the hours of this heaven-appointed day of rest and religious improvement may be spent in a manner profitable to ourselves and well-pleasing in the sight of that gracious Being who says by the mouth of the prophet, *If thou turn away thy foot from the Sabbath, from doing thy pleasure on my holy day; and call the Sabbath a delight, the holy of the Lord, honorable; and shalt honor him, not doing thine own ways, nor finding thine own pleasure, nor speaking thine own words: then shalt thou delight thyself in the Lord; and I will cause thee to ride upon the high places of the earth, and feed thee with the heritage of Jacob thy father: for the mouth of the Lord hath spoken it.* Isa. lviii, 13, 14.

QUESTIONS ON LESSON L.

1. Can you repeat the passage quoted from Hosea?
2. How is it explained?
3. Who refers to the passage?
4. For what does Jesus rebuke the Jews?
5. Why did the Jews accuse Christ of breaking the Sabbath?
6. What did Jesus teach by precept and by example?
7. To what do these deeds of mercy refer?
8. What is here said to be an act of mercy?
9. What is the teaching of Luke xiv, 5?
10. Repeat Matthew xii, 12.
11. Why is a caution necessary?
12. What may be made a pretense for neglecting Sabbath duties?
13. How is this illustrated?
14. On whom may we impose by this conduct?
15. Who will not be deceived?
16. What is the second caution here given?
17. What is said of idleness?
18. What is said of the Sabbath as a day of rest?
19. What cannot imagination picture?
20. What is the third class of Sabbath duties?
21. What is said of the acquisition of divine knowledge?
22. With what are we abundantly furnished?
23. What is said of the Bible and other books?
24. What is said of the family circle and the Sunday-school?
25. Can you repeat the passage from Isaiah?

LESSON FIFTY-FIRST.

DIVINE WORSHIP.

Religious worship of some kind seems to be an instinct of human nature. There are few if any of the various tribes of men which do not acknowledge and pay some sort of homage to what they deem superior beings, real or imaginary. It is our privilege to live in a land which is full of light from heaven beaming from the sacred Scriptures, and the Bible makes known to us the existence and the attributes of the true God, and teaches us how he is to be worshiped.

First, of course, in sincerity. So Christ taught the woman at Jacob's well. *God is a spirit; and they that worship him must worship him in spirit and in truth.* John iv, 24. So too reason teaches. To him who knoweth all things, even the secret thoughts of every creature, it is evident that nothing but sincerity can be acceptable, and that pretended worship, while it may deceive every other being in the universe, cannot for a moment impose upon Him who looketh upon the heart. 1 Sam. xvi, 7.

In the second place the worship of God always includes thanksgiving, or expressions of gratitude. The psalmist says, *Offer unto God thanksgiving;* and He declares that *whoso offereth praise glorifieth me.* Psa. l, 14, 23. We need not look far to find reasons for thanksgiving. God gave us being. He preserves our lives, our health, our reason. In short, we are indebted to him for all we have, for all we are, for all we hope to be. Instinctively we thank a fellow-creature for a favor conferred upon us, and in proportion to the value of that favor is the gratitude excited. So should it be toward our heavenly Father. But so to a very great extent it is not. Multitudes never think of sincerely thanking God for the blessings they enjoy.

Hence, thirdly, acceptable worship includes the confession of past ingratitude, and of course of all other past offenses. This, also, is equally the dictate of reason and of Scripture. If a child has done wrong, and offended his parents or teacher, his first duty is to acknowledge that wrong. It is not possible that his thanks for present favors can be sincere, (and if not sincere they cannot be acceptable,) unless he first confess his wrong-doing. So our heavenly Father, by the prophet Hosea, (v, 15,) says, *I will go and return to my place till they acknowledge their offense;* intimating that without such acknowledgment they would seek his face in vain, and of course could not worship him acceptably. Hence the promise of mercy is to him who *confesseth and forsaketh his sins.* Prov. xxviii, 13. And hence the exclamation of the psalmist: *I acknowledge my transgressions, and my sin is ever before me.* Psa. li, 3.

The fourth and last form of religious worship that we shall mention as among the duties we owe to our Maker is that of prayer. The apostle says, (Phil. iv, 6,) *Let your requests be made known unto God;* and Jesus says, *Men ought always to pray.* Luke xviii, 1. Here are indicated two things: first, they err who teach that prayer to be acceptable can only be offered in a prescribed form, or in language prepared for the purpose. He who can make known a request can pray, and is invited to do so, and is indeed guilty of neglecting a duty so long as he continues to neglect prayer. Secondly: it is a mistake to suppose that none but Christians have a right to pray.

Jesus says, *Men*, human beings, all, young and old, *ought to pray*. *You* ought to pray. It is as much your duty as it is the duty of any other human being. Until it may be said of you as it was of Saul of Tarsus, *Behold he prayeth*, (Acts ix, 11,) but little good may be expected from your studies of moral science. Its requirements will seem unpleasant and very frequently impracticable. On the other hand, with the assisting grace of our Lord Jesus Christ—and that is to be had only in answer to prayer—the moral duties enjoined upon you will be pleasant and easy.

Questions on Lesson LI.

1. What is said of religious worship?
2. To whom do almost all men pay some sort of homage?
3. What is said of the land we live in?
4. What beams from the sacred Scriptures?
5. Whence do we get knowledge as to how God is to be worshiped?
6. What is the first element of true worship?
7. Can you give the substance of what passed between Christ and the Samaritan woman, as found in John iv?

8. What else teaches the importance of sincerity in worship?
9. What Scripture is there for thanksgiving as a duty to God?
10. Can you name some causes for thanksgiving?
11. What is said of multitudes?
12. What is next said to be included in acceptable worship?
13. How does reason indicate this duty?
14. What is said in Hosea v, 15?
15. What do you understand by that?
16. To whom is the promise of mercy made in Prov. xxviii, 13?
17. What duty is next mentioned?
18. Repeat Philippians iv, 6.
19. Who says men ought always to pray?
20. What two errors are exposed here?

FIFTY-SECOND LESSON.

FOURTH QUARTERLY REVISION.

We have now reached the last week of the last quarter, and for to-day's lesson we review the studies of the preceding three months. As on former quarterly reviews, the questions to be asked may, for the most part, be answered by referring to the preceding lessons.

1. When and by whom was marriage instituted?
2. Repeat what Jesus Christ says in Matt. xix, 4, 6.
3. What is said of the company of the impure?
4. Discriminate between an untruth, a falsehood, and a lie.
5. Illustrate how the guilt of a lie may be incurred without speaking.
6. How can the guilt of falsehood be incurred if no one is deceived?
7. Who was Gehazi, and what punishment was inflicted upon him?
8. Who was Plato, and where did he live?
9. Relate what you know about the Jesuits.
10. Who was Origen?
11. By what name do the Roman Catholics call Protestant Christians?
12. What are an abomination to the Lord?
13. Where shall all liars have their part?
14. What are the only justifications for not fullfilling a promise?
15. Who was Regulus?
16. What may the conduct of Regulus teach us?

17. What do you understand by prevarication?
18. Can you give an instance of prevarication?
19. Give an illustration of deception by equivocation.
20. What was the peculiar trait in the character of a young lady by which she acquired the name of Miss Superlative?
21. What does Solomon say worketh ruin?
22. What is called one of the meanest vices?
23. Quote the passages from the Bible which refer to tale-bearing.
24. How may we share the guilt of a slanderer without saying anything?
25. What aggravates the guilt of perjury beyond that of lying?
26. What is the commandment with threatening?
27. State some of the methods by which that command is violated.
28. Why is an oath in a court of justice necessary?
29. What are the two methods by which judicial oaths are taken?
30. What is the teaching of Jesus Christ on the subject of profaneness?

31. With what sins is swearing classed by the prophet Hosea?
32. On what account does the prophet Jeremiah say the land mourneth?
33. In what respect does swearing differ from other acts of transgression?
34. Whence arises the pleasure of taking God's name in vain?
35. What will be the probable fate of the profane swearer?
36. How are boys led into the habit of swearing?
37. Which of the commandments relates to the Sabbath day?
38. On what day of the week was the Sabbath originally kept?
39. On what day is it now kept by Christians?
40. When, why, and by whom was the day changed?
41. How do you prove that the Sabbath is a type of heaven?
42. State some things that may be done on the Lord's day.
43. Mention some things that ought not to be done on that day.
44. How do you prove that acts of mercy may be performed on the Lord's day?

45. Is idleness justifiable on the Sabbath?
46. What is said to be an instinct of human nature?
47. Whence do we obtain our knowledge of the manner in which God is to be worshiped?
48. Mention some passages of Scripture which prove thanksgiving to be a religious duty.
49. How do you prove it to be a duty to confess our sins?
50. Who ought to pray?

THE END.

VOLCANOES:

Their History, Phenomena, and Causes. 18mo., pp. 233. Price, 25 cents.

THE CLASS OF A-THOUSAND-AND-ONE.

A Sunday-School Memorial. 18mo., pp. 92. Price, 16 cents.

MARGARET BROWNING;

Or, Trust in God. Four Illustrations. 18mo., pp. 147. Price, 20 cents.

THOUGHTS OF HEAVEN.

By the Author of "The Prince Family," "Dying Hours," etc. 18mo., pp. 154. Price, 20 cents.

TORTOLA;

Or, the Native Missionary. Two Illustrations. 18mo., pp. 120. Price, 18 cents.

RECOLLECTIONS OF WM. THEOPHILUS,

A Pilgrim of Fourscore. Four Illustrations. 18mo., pp. 152. Price, 20 cents.

MONEY MATTERS

Explained to the Young. By Rev. L. L. Knox. Five Illustrations. 18mo., pp. 132. Price, 18 cents.

SUNDAY HOURS.

A Book for Young People. Five Illustrations. 18mo., pp. 181. Price, 22 cents.

FRANK NETHERTON;

Or, the Talisman. Five Illustrations. 18mo., pp. 234. Price, 25 cents.

THE GREAT EXHIBITION.

By the Editor of "Pleasant Pages." Six Illustrations. 18mo., pp. 222. Price, 24 cents.

REMARKABLE DELUSIONS;

Or, Illustrations of Popular Errors. 18mo., pp. 218. Price, 24 cents.

200 Mulberry-street, New York.

LETTERS TO LITTLE CHILDREN.

Seven Illustrations. 18mo., pp. 110. Price, 18 cents

BE PATIENT;

Or, The Story of Solomon Granby, related by Himself 18mo., pp. 90. Price, 16 cents.

AN EXAMPLE FOR YOUNG MEN:

A Memoir of John Daglish. By SAMUEL DUNN. 18mo., pp. 92. Price, 17 cents.

PITHY PAPERS,

For Week-Day Reading. By OLD HUMPHREY. Three Illustrations. 18mo., pp. 219. Price, 24 cents.

SODOM AND GOMORRAH.

A Brief Account of Sodom and Gomorrah. Two Illustrations. 18mo., pp. 63. Price, 15 cents.

THE FEAST OF BELSHAZZAR.

By the Author of "Sodom and Gomorrah." 18mo., pp. 56. Price, 14 cents.

APPEARANCE AND PRINCIPLE;

Or, A Sketch of Three Young Ladies at School, and in Subsequent Life. 18mo., pp. 56. Price, 14 cents.

THE WILL-FORGERS;

Or, The Church of Rome. By Rev. C. B. TAYLER. 18mo., pp. 99. Price, 17 cents.

THE WIDOW'S JEWELS.

By MRS. PICKARD. Two Illustrations. 18mo., pp. 64. Price, 15 cents.

THE STORY OF JEROBOAM,

The Son of Nebat. By WILLIAM A. ALCOTT. 18mo., pp. 85. Price, 16 cents.

THE VISITOR;

Or, Calls of Usefulness. Illustrated. Two volumes, 18mo., pp. 105, 94. Price, 35 cents.

WAYSIDE FRAGMENTS;

Or, Wonders in Common Things. By the Author of "Peeps at Nature," "Nature's Wonders," "Village Science," etc. Twelve Illustrations. 18mo., pp. 204. Price, 23 cents.

TYRE:

Its Rise, Glory, and Desolation. With Notices of the Phœnicians generally. 18mo., pp. 214. Price, 24 cents.

SARAH NEAL.

A Tale of Real Life. By the Author of "Roland Rand" and "The Homely Child." Three Illustrations. 18mo., pp. 76. Price, 15 cents

MY FIRST SEVEN YEARS IN AMERICA.

By Rev. George Coles, late Assistant Editor of the Christian Advocate and Journal, Author of "Lectures to Children," etc. 18mo., pp. 314. Price, 30 cents.

LIFE OF REV. ENOCH GEORGE,

One of the Bishops of the M. E. Church. By Benjamin St. James Fry. 18mo., pp. 124. Price, 18 cents.

LIFE OF REV. WILLIAM M'KENDREE,

One of the Bishops of the M. E. Church. By Benjamin St. James Fry. 18mo., pp. 197. Price, 22 cents.

LIFE OF REV. RICHARD WHATCOAT,

One of the Bishops of the M. E. Church. By Benjamin St. James Fry. 18mo., pp. 128. Price, 18 cents.

AUNT EFFIE;

Or, the Pious Widow and her Infidel Brother. By Rev. Daniel Wise, author of "Guide to the Saviour," "Path of Life," "Young Man's Counselor," etc. Two Illustrations. 18mo., pp. 174. Price, 22 cents.

BE COURTEOUS;

Or, Religion the True Refiner. By Mrs. M. H. Maxwell. Three Illustrations. 18mo., pp. 183. Price, 22 cents.

BOOKS FOR SUNDAY SCHOOLS.

200 Mulberry-street, New-York.

MEMOIR OF OLD HUMPHREY;

With Gleanings from his Portfolio, in Prose and Verse. Two Illustrations. 18mo., pp. 298. Price, 35 cents.

THE HAPPY RESOLVE.

A Tale from Real Life. 18mo., pp. 78. Price, 16 cents.

THE YOUTH'S MONITOR.

Volume IV. 18mo., pp. 288. Price, 28 cents.

THE PROMPTER;

Or, The Sunday Scholar's True Friend. Volume II. 18mo., pp. 288. Price, 28 cents.

THE CHILD'S PREACHER:

A Series of Addresses to the Young. Founded on Scripture Texts. 18mo., pp. 451. Price, 45 cents.

BLOOMING HOPES

And Withered Joys. By Rev. J. T. Barr, author of "Recollections of a Minister," "Merchant's Daughter," etc. Five Illustrations. 18mo., pp. 286. Price, 35 cents.

THE EARLY DEAD;

Containing Brief Memoirs of Sunday-School Children. Volume IV. 18mo., pp. 224. Price, 25 cents.

JOHNNY M'KAY;

Or, the Sovereign: the Story of an Honest Boy Five Illustrations. 18mo., pp. 220. Price, 30 cents

ADDIE OAKLAND;

Or, Charity the True Road to Happiness. Six Illustrations. 18mo., pp. 136. Price, 22 cents.

IRISH STORIES,

For Thoughtful Readers. Five Illustrations. 18mo pp. 285. Price, 32 cents.

LITTLE WATER-CRESS SELLERS.

18mo., pp. 80. Price, 16 cents.

200 Mulberry-street, New-York.

SOCIAL PROGRESS;

Or, Business and Pleasure. By the Author of "Nature's Wonders," "Village Science," etc. Sixteen Illustrations. 18mo., pp. 269. Price, 35 cents.

GREEK AND EASTERN CHURCHES:

Their History, Faith, and Worship. 18mo., pp. 220. Price, 25 cents.

The Greek Church is a great phenomenon, full of interest to the statesman, scholar, theologian, and the educated classes.

SUCCESSFUL MEN OF MODERN TIMES.

18mo., pp. 207. Price, 25 cents.

CHEERFUL CHAPTERS:

Adapted to Youth, and not unsuited to Age. By old Alan Gray. Four Illustrations. 18mo., pp. 179. Price, 25 cents.

THE KITTEN IN THE WELL;

Or, one Sinner destroyeth much Good. By Father William. Four Illustrations. 18mo., pp. 84. Price, 16 cents.

MARCEY, THE APPLE-WOMAN'S SON.

A true Narrative. Two Illustrations. 18mo., pp. 54. Price, 13 cents.

THREE DAYS ON THE OHIO RIVER.

By Father William. Two Illustrations. 18mo., pp. 60. Price, 15 cents.

MARY SEFTON;

The Orphan Governess. Three Illustrations. 18mo., pp. 86. Price, 16 cents.

LIFE OF ALEXANDER THE GREAT.

18mo., pp. 208. Price, 25 cents.

SKETCHES OF MISSION LIFE

Among the Indians of Oregon. Five Illustrations. 18mo., pp. 229. Price, 28 cents.

200 Mulberry-street, New York.

THE LIFE OF ESTHER.

By Rev. DANIEL SMITH. 18mo. Price, 18 cents.

LIFE OF ADAM CLARKE.

An Account of the Religious and Literary Life of Rev Adam Clarke, LL.D. 18mo. Price, 24 cents.

LIFE OF JOHN THE BAPTIST.

By Rev. DANIEL SMITH. 18mo. Price, 17 cents.

LIFE OF MRS. COKE.

Memoir of Mrs. Penelope Goulding Coke, by her Husband, the late Rev. DR. COKE. 18mo. Price, 16 cents.

THE LIFE OF ABRAHAM.

By Rev. DANIEL SMITH. 18mo. Price, 19 cents.

THE LIFE OF SAMSON.

By Rev. DANIEL SMITH. 18mo. Price, 16 cents.

THE THEOLOGICAL COMPEND:

Containing a System of Divinity, or a brief View of the Evidences, Doctrines, Morals, and Institutions of Christianity. Designed for the benefit of Families, Bible Classes, and Sunday Schools. By AMOS BINNEY. 18mo. Price, 19 cents.

THE LIFE OF JONAH.

By Rev. DANIEL SMITH. Two Illustrations. 18mo. Price, 16 cents.

CONVERSATIONS ON PALESTINE.

Conversations on the Geography, Natural History, etc., of Palestine. By IMOGEN MERCEIN. Illustrated. 18mo. Price, 29 cents.

MORAL FABLES AND PARABLES.

By INGRAM COBBIN, M. A. Illustrated. 18mo. Price, 16 cents.

STORIES FROM HISTORY OF SCOTLAND.

By Rev. ALEXANDER STEWART, a Minister of that Country. 18mo. Price, 21 cents.

BOOKS FOR SUNDAY SCHOOLS.

200 Mulberry-street, New-York.

MIRIAM GREY;

Or, Scenes from the True History of a Life. 18mo., pp. 56. Price, 15 cents.

THE PROMPTER;

Or, the Sunday Scholar's true Friend. Vol. I. 18mo., pp. 288. Price, 28 cents.

THE SUNDAY SHOP;

Or, the Fourth Commandment. 18mo., pp. 74. Price, 16 cents.

INCIDENTS OF MY LATER YEARS:

A Sequel to "My Youthful Days," and "My First Seven Years in America." By Rev. George Coles. 18mo., pp. 315. Price, 30 cents.

THE THANKFUL WIDOW.

18mo., pp. 46. Price, 13 cents.

LIFE OF ROBERT R. ROBERTS,

One of the Bishops of the Methodist Episcopal Church. By Benjamin St. James Fry. 18mo., pp. 126. Price, 20 cents.

SUMMER MEMORIES.

Long Branch and Wilderstein. By the Author of "Little Ella," "The Beatitudes," etc. Three Illustrations. 18mo., pp. 142. Price, 22 cents.

ELLEN AND SARAH;

Or, The Samplers. And other Stories. Eight Illustrations. 18mo., pp. 204. Price, 30 cents.

THE CONTRAST;

Or, Two Young Men described by an Acquaintance. Five Illustrations. 18mo., pp. 154. Price, 25 cents.

STORIES FOR VILLAGE LADS.

By the Author of "Stories of School-Boys," "Frank Harrison," etc., etc. Four Illustrations. 18mo., pp 176. Price, 25 cents.

BOOKS FOR SUNDAY SCHOOLS.

200 Mulberry-street, New York.

THE GIPSY IN ALL NATIONS.

Four Illustrations. 18mo., pp. 172. Price, 22 cents.

WRITTEN PICTURES;

Or, Short Talks to Young People. By a Teacher. 18mo., pp. 91. Price, 17 cents.

BE DILIGENT:

An Important Precept practically illustrated. Two Illustrations. 18mo., pp. 107. Price, 18 cents.

THE CRUSADES.

18mo., pp. 224. Price, 24 cents.

DWELLERS ON THE HOLY HILL;

Or, Familiar Illustrations of the Characters described in the Fifteenth Psalm. 18mo., pp. 103. Price, 18 cents.

LESSONS OF A DISCIPLE;

Or, Chapters in the Life of a Young Lady. 18mo., pp. 103. Price, 18 cents.

THE NOBLE CONVERT.

Reminiscences of the West India Islands, No. I. 18mo., pp. 66. Price, 15 cents.

THE PERSECUTING GOVERNOR.

Reminiscences of the West India Islands, No. II. 18mo., pp. 92. Price, 16 cents.

THE IMPRISONED COOPER.

Reminiscences of the West India Islands, No. III. 18mo., pp. 68. Price, 15 cents.

THE BEREAVED WIDOW.

Reminiscences of the West India Islands, No. IV 18mo., pp. 82. Price, 16 cents.

JACK RAY, THE CONVERTED SLAVE.

Reminiscences of the West India Islands, No. V 18mo., pp. 88. Price, 16 cents.

MAGIC,

Pretended Miracles, and Remarkable Natural Phenomena. Illustrated. 18mo., pp. 217. Price, 24 cents.

PROCRASTINATION;

Or, Maria Louisa Winslow. By MRS. H. M. PICKARD. 18mo., pp. 116. Price, 18 cents.

CHRISTIAN PEACE;

Or, The Third Fruit of the Spirit. Illustrated by Scenes from Real Life. 18mo., pp. 128. Price, 19 cents.

THE CAVES OF THE EARTH:

Their Natural History, Features and Incidents. 18mo., pp. 187. Price, 22 cents.

THE BLIND MAN'S SON;

Or, The Poor Student successfully struggling to overcome Adversity and Misfortune. Two Illustrations. 18mo., pp. 270. Price, 27 cents.

THE EARLY DEAD:

Containing Brief Memoirs of Sunday-School Children. Three volumes, 18mo., pp. 92, 98, 158. Price, 53 cents.

HOSTETLER;

Or, The Mennonite Boy converted. A true Narrative By a Methodist Preacher. Two Illustrations. 18mo., pp. 138. Price, 19 cents.

MOUNTAINS OF THE BIBLE.

Conversations on the Mountains of the Bible, and the Scenes and Circumstances connected with them in Holy Writ. Supplementary to the "Mountains of the Pentateuch." By E. M. B. Four Illustrations. 18mo., pp. 265. Price, 23 cents.

ANGEL WHISPERS;

Or, The Story of Thomas and Edward. Two Illustrations. 18mo., pp. 78. Price, 15 cents.

BOOKS FOR SUNDAY SCHOOLS.

200 Mulberry-street, New York.

MEMOIRS OF JOHN FREDERIC OBERLIN

Pastor of Waldbach, in the Ban De La Roche. 18mo Price, 23 cents.

SCRIPTURE PROPHECY.

Fulfillment of Scripture Prophecy, as Exhibited in Ancient History and Modern Travels. By STEPHEN B. WICKENS. Three Illustrations. 18mo. Price, 30 cents.

MEMOIRS OF THE LATE JANE TAYLOR.

By ISAAC TAYLOR. With a brief Introduction, by Rev DANIEL SMITH. 18mo. Price, 18 cents.

LIFE OF SOLOMON, KING OF ISRAEL:

By Rev. DANIEL SMITH. Four Illustrations. 18mo Price, 20 cents.

LIFE OF THE APOSTLE JOHN.

By Rev. DANIEL SMITH. 18mo. Price, 24 cents.

THE LIFE OF HEZEKIAH.

By Rev. DANIEL SMITH. 18mo. Price, 15 cents.

DEAF AND DUMB.

Recollections of the Deaf and Dumb. 18mo. Price, 18 cents.

HISTORY OF THE PATRIARCH JACOB.

By Rev. DANIEL SMITH. Five Illustrations. 18mo Price, 22 cents.

THE WATERLOO SOLDIER.

Three Illustrations. 18mo. Price, 14 cents.

THE LIFE OF JOSHUA.

By Rev. DANIEL SMITH. Three Illustrations. 18mo Price, 22 cents.

THE LIFE OF ELIJAH.

By Rev. DANIEL SMITH. Five Illustrations. 18mo Price, 21 cents.

200 Mulberry-street, New-York.

THE TEMPEST;

Or, an Account of the Nature, Properties, Dangers and Uses of Wind in various parts of the World. Fourteen Illustrations. 18mo., pp. 230. Price, 28 cents.

THE YOUTH'S MONITOR.

Vols. I, II, III. 18mo., pp. 288. Price, 28 cents each.

OLD CRAG;

Or, the Alison Family. An Authentic Tale of Rural and Factory Life. By a Minister. Five Illustrations. 18mo., pp. 216. Price, 25 cents.

RAMBLES IN THE SOUTH.

Recollections of Rambles in the South. By FATHER WILLIAM. Five Illustrations. 18mo., pp. 196. Price, 25 cents.

KENNETH FORBES;

Or, Fourteen Ways of Studying the Bible. Seven Illustrations. 18mo., pp. 298. Price, 32 cents.

THE LAMP AND THE LANTERN;

Or, Light for the Tent and the Traveler. By JAMES HAMILTON, D.D. 18mo., pp. 202. Price, 23 cents.

THREE MONTHS UNDER THE SNOW.

The Journal of a Young Inhabitant of the Jura. Translated from the French of J. J. PORCHAT. Four Illustrations. 18mo., pp. 178. Price, 22 cents.

CHARLES ROUSSEL;

Or, Industry and Honesty. Adapted from the French of J. J. PORCHAT, author of "Three Months under the Snow." By Rev. T. T. HAVERFIELD. Three Illustrations. 18mo., pp. 224. Price, 25 cents.

JAMES BAIRD;

Or, the Basket Maker's Son. By the Author of "Father Johnson," "Thoughts of Heaven," "Prince Family," etc. Four Illustrations. 18mo., pp. 144. Price, 22 cents.

200 Mulberry-street, New York.

THE MISSIONARY TEACHER:

A Memoir of Cyrus Shepard, embracing a Brief Sketch of the Early History of the Oregon Mission. By Rev. Z. A. MUDGE. Seven Illustrations. 18mo., pp. 221. Price, 24 cents.

BE GOOD:

An Important Precept illustrated in Ralph's Account of a Visit to the Country. Four Illustrations. 18mo., pp. 60. Price, 14 cents.

HADASSAH;

Or, The Adopted Child. Two Illustrations. 18mo., pp. 112. Price, 18 cents.

THE LIVES OF THE CÆSARS.

For Week-day Reading. Six Illustrations. 18mo., pp. 221. Price, 24 cents.

THE LIFE OF MOHAMMED.

Three Illustrations. 18mo., pp. 184. Price, 22 cents.

THE HIGHLAND GLEN;

Or, Plenty and Famine. Two Illustrations. 18mo., pp. 70. Price, 15 cents.

FEMALE SUNDAY SCHOLAR.

Parting Precepts to a Female Sunday Scholar on her Advantages and Responsibilities. By MRS. J. BAKEWELL. 18mo., pp. 96. Price, 17 cents.

NEDDY WALTER;

Or, The Wilderness made to Bloom. Two Illustrations. 18mo., pp. 102. Price, 16 cents.

HARRIET GRAY;

Or, The Selfish Girl cured. 18mo., pp. 80. Price, 16 cents.

CUBA.

By Rev. JAMES RAWSON, A. M. Illustrated. 18mo., pp. 70. Price, 15 cents.